PENGUIN BOOKS

TZILI

Aharon Appelfeld was born in Czernovitz, Bukovina (now part of the U.S.S.R.), in 1932. At eight he was sent by the Nazis to a concentration camp, but he escaped and spent the next three years hiding in the Ukrainian countryside before joining the Russian army. A refugee after the war, he soon made his way to Italy and, in 1946, to Palestine. He now lives in Jerusalem. His published works in Hebrew include six collections of stories, a book of essays, and seven novels, of which *Tzili* is the third to be published in English, following the critically acclaimed *Badenheim 1939* and *The Age of Wonders*.

TZILI

The Story of a Life

◆ ◆ ◆

Aharon Appelfeld

◆

Translated by Dalya Bilu

PENGUIN BOOKS

Penguin Books Ltd, Harmondsworth,
Middlesex, England
Penguin Books, 40 West 23rd Street,
New York, New York 10010, U.S.A.
Penguin Books Australia Ltd, Ringwood,
Victoria, Australia
Penguin Books Canada Limited, 2801 John Street,
Markham, Ontario, Canada L3R 1B4
Penguin Books (N.Z.) Ltd, 182–190 Wairau Road,
Auckland 10, New Zealand

First published in the United States of America by
E. P. Dutton, Inc., 1983
Published in Penguin Books 1984

LIBRARY OF CONGRESS CATALOGING IN PUBLICATION DATA
Appelfeld, Aharon.
Tzili, the story of a life.
1. Holocaust, Jewish (1939–1945)—Fiction.
I. Title.
PJ5054.A755T9   1984   892.4′36   83-24991
ISBN 0 14 00.7058 3

Printed in the United States of America by
R. R. Donnelley & Sons Company, Harrisonburg, Virginia
Set in Melior

This novel was first serialized in *Molad*, in Israel,
in the spring of 1982.

TZILI
The Story of a Life

1

Perhaps it would be better to leave the story of Tzili Kraus's life untold. Her fate was a cruel and inglorious one, and but for the fact that it actually happened we would never have been able to tell her story. We will tell it in all simplicity, and begin right away by saying: Tzili was not an only child; she had older brothers and sisters. The family was large, poor, and harassed, and Tzili grew up neglected among the abandoned objects in the yard.

Her father was an invalid and her mother busy all day long in their little shop. In the evening, sometimes without even thinking, one of her brothers or sisters would pick her out of the dirt and take her into the house. She was a quiet creature, devoid of charm and almost mute. Tzili would get up early in the morning and go to bed at night like a squirrel, without complaints or tears.

And thus she grew. Most of the summer and autumn she spent out of doors. In winter she snuggled into her pillows. Since she was small and skinny and didn't get in anyone's way, they ignored her existence. Every now and then her mother would remember her and cry: "Tzili, where are you?" "Here." The answer would not be long in coming, and the mother's sudden panic would pass.

When she was seven years old they sewed her a satchel, bought her two copybooks, and sent her to school. It was a country school, built of gray stone and covered with a tiled roof. In this building she studied for five years. Unlike other members of her race, Tzili did not shine at school. She was clumsy and somewhat withdrawn. The big letters on the blackboard made her head spin. At the end of the first term there was no longer any doubt: Tzili was dull-witted. The mother was busy and harassed but she gave vent to her anger nevertheless: "You must work harder. Why don't you work harder?" The sick father, hearing the mother's threats, sighed in his bed: What was to become of them?

Tzili would learn things by heart and immediately forget them again. Even the gentile children knew more than she did. She would get mixed up. A Jewish girl without any brains! They delighted in her misfortune. Tzili would promise herself not to get mixed up, but the moment she stood in front of the blackboard the words vanished and her hands froze.

For hours she sat and studied. But all her efforts didn't help her. In the fourth grade she still hadn't mastered the multiplication table and her hand-writing was vague and confused. Sometimes her mother lost her temper and hit her. The sick father was no gentler than the mother. He would call her and ask: "Why don't you study?"

"I do study."

"Why don't you know anything?"

Tzili would hang her head.

"Why are you bringing this disgrace on your family?" He would grind his teeth.

The father's illness was fatal, but the dull presence of his youngest daughter hurt him more than his wound. Again and again he blamed her laziness, her unwillingness, but never her inability. "If you want to you can." This wasn't a judgment, but a faith. In this faith they were all united, the mother in the shop and her daughters at their books.

Tzili's brothers and sisters all worked with a will. They prepared for external examinations, registered for crash courses, devoured supplementary material. Tzili cooked, washed dishes, and weeded the garden. She was small and thin, and kneeling in the garden she looked like a servant girl.

But all her hard work did not save her from her disgrace. Again and again: "Why don't you know anything? Even the gentile children know more than you do." The riddle of Tzili's failure tortured everyone, but especially the mother. From time to time a deep groan burst from her chest, as if she were mourning a premature death.

In the winter evil rumors were already rife, but only echoes reached the remoter districts. The Kraus family labored like ants. They hoarded food, the daughters memorized dates, the younger son drew clumsy geometric figures on long sheets of paper. The examinations were imminent, and they cast their shadow over everyone. Heavy sighs emerged from the father's darkened room: "Study, children, study. Don't be lazy." The vestiges of a liturgical chant in his voice aroused his daughters' ire.

At home Tzili was sometimes forgotten, but at school, among all the gentile children, she was the butt of constant ridicule and scorn. Strange: she never cried or begged for mercy. Every day she went to her torture chamber and swallowed the dose of insults meted out to her.

Once a week a tutor came from the village to teach her her prayers. The family no longer observed the rituals of the Jewish religion, but her mother for some reason got it into her head that religious study would be good for Tzili, besides putting a little money the old man's way. The tutor came on different days of the week, in the afternoons. He never raised his voice to Tzili. For the first hour he would tell her stories from the Bible and for the second he would read the prayer book with her. At the end of the lesson she would make him a cup of tea. "How is the child progressing?" the mother would ask every now and then. "She's a good girl," the old man would say. He knew that the family did not keep the Sabbath or pray, and he wondered why it had fallen to the lot of this dull child to keep the spark alive. Tzili did her best to please the old man, but as far as reading was concerned her progress left much to be desired. Among her brothers and sisters the old man's visits gave rise to indignation. He wore a white coat and shabby shoes, and his eyes glinted with the skepticism of a man whose scholarship had not helped him in his hour of need. His sons had emigrated to America, and he was left alone in the derelict old house. He knew that he was nothing but a lackey in the service of Tzili's family's hysteria, and that her brothers and sisters could not bear his presence in the house. He swallowed his humiliation quietly, but not without disgust.

At the end of the reading in the prayer book he would ask Tzili, in the traditional, unvarying formula:

"What is man?"

And Tzili would reply: "Dust and ashes."

"And before whom is he destined to stand in judgment?"

"Before the King of Kings, the Holy One blessed be He."

"And what must he do?"

"Pray and observe the commandments of the Torah."

"And where are the commandments of the Torah written?"

"In the Torah."

This set formula, spoken in a kind of lilt, would awaken loud echoes in Tzili's soul, and their reverberations spread throughout her body. Strange: Tzili was not afraid of the old man. His visits filled her with a kind of serenity which remained with her and protected her for many hours afterward. At night she would recite "Hear, O Israel" aloud, as he had instructed her, covering her face.

And thus she grew. But for the old man's visits her life would have been even more wretched. She learned to take up as little space as possible. She even went to the lavatory in secret, so as not to draw attention to herself. The old man, to tell the truth, felt no affection for her. From time to time he grew impatient and scolded her, but she liked listening to his voice and imagined that she heard tenderness in it.

2

When the war broke out they all ran away, leaving Tzili to look after the house. They thought nobody would harm a feeble-minded little girl, and until the storm had spent itself, she could take care of their property for them. Tzili heard their verdict without protest. They left in a panic, without time for second thoughts. "We'll come back for you later," said her brothers as they lifted their father onto the stretcher. And thus they parted from her.

That same night the soldiers invaded the town and destroyed it. A terrible wailing rose into the air. But Tzili, for some reason, escaped unharmed. Perhaps they didn't see her. She lay in the yard, among the barrels in the shed, covered with sacking. She knew that she had to look after the house, but her fear stopped her from doing so. Secretly she hoped for the sound of a familiar voice coming to call her. The air was full of loud screams, barks, and shots. In her fear she repeated the words she had been taught by the old man, over and over again. The mumbled words calmed her and she fell asleep.

She slept for a long time. When she woke it was night and everything was completely still. She poked her head out of the sacking, and the night sky appeared through the cracks in the roof of the shed. She lifted the upper half of her body, propping herself up on her elbows. Her feet were numb with cold. She passed both hands over the round columns of her legs and rubbed them. A pain shot through her feet.

For a long time she lay supporting herself on her elbows, looking at the sky. And while she lay listening, her lips parted and mumbled:

"Before whom is he destined to stand in judgment?"

"Before the King of Kings, the Holy One blessed be He."

The old man had insisted on the proper pronunciation of the words, and it was this insistence she remembered now.

But in the meantime the numbness left her legs, and she kicked away the sacking. She said to herself: "I must get up," and she stood up. The shed was much higher than she was. It was made of rough planks and used to store wood, barrels, an old bathtub, and a few earthenware pots. No one but Tzili paid any attention to this old shed, but for her it was a hiding place. Now she felt a kind of intimacy with the abandoned objects lying in it.

For the first time she found herself under the open night sky. When she was a baby they would close the shutters very early, and later on, when she grew up, they never let her go outside in the dark. For the first time she touched the darkness with her fingers.

She turned right, into the open fields. The sky suddenly grew taller, and she was small next to the standing corn. For a long time she walked without turning her head. Afterward she stopped and listened to the rustle of the leaves. A light breeze blew and the cool darkness assuaged her thirst a little.

On either side stretched crowded cornfields, one plot next to the other, with here and there a fence. Once or twice she stumbled and fell but she immediately rose to her feet again. In the end she hitched her dress up and tucked it into her belt, and this immediately liberated her legs. From now on she walked easily.

For some reason she began to run. A memory invaded her and frightened her. The memory was so dim that after she ran a little way it disappeared. She resumed her previous pace.

Her oldest sister, who was preparing for examinations, was the worst of them all. When she was swotting, she would chase Tzili away without even lifting her head from her books. Tzili loved her sister and the harsh words hurt her. Once her sister had said: "Get out of my sight. I never want to see you again. You make me nervous." Strange: these words rather than any others were the ones that seemed to carve themselves out of the darkness.

The darkness seeped slowly away. A few pale stripes appeared in the sky and turned a deeper pink. Tzili bent over to rub her feet and sat down. Unthinkingly she sank her teeth into a cornstalk. A stream of cool liquid washed her throat.

The light broke above her and poured onto her head. A few solitary animal cries drifted through the valley and a loud chorus of barks immediately rose to join them. She sat and listened. The distant sounds cradled her. Without thinking she fell asleep.

The sun warmed her body and she slept for many hours. When she woke she was bathed in sweat. She picked up her dress and shook off the grains of sand sticking to her skin. The sun caressed her limbs and for the first time she felt the sweet pain of being alone.

And while everything was still quiet and wrapped in shadows a shot pierced the air, followed by a sharp, interrupted scream. She bent down and covered her face. For a long time she did not lift her head. Now it seemed to her that something had happened to her body, in the region of the chest, but it was only a vague, hollow numbness after a day without eating.

The sun sank and Tzili saw her father lying on his bed. The last days at home, the rumors and the panic. Books and copybooks. No one showed any consideration for the feelings of his fellows. The examinations, which were to take place shortly in the distant town, threatened them all, especially her oldest sister. She tore out her hair in despair. Their mother too, in the shop, between one customer and the next, appeared to be repeating dates and formulas to herself. The truth was that she was angry. Only the sick father lay calmly in his bed. As if he had succeeded in steering the household onto the right course. He seemed to have forgotten his illness, perhaps even the dull presence of his youngest daughter. What he had failed to accomplish in his own life his children would accomplish for him: they would study. They would bring diplomas home.

And with these sights before her eyes she fell asleep.

3

When she woke, her memory was empty and weightless. She rose and left the cornfield and made for the outskirts of the forest. As if to spite her, another picture rose before her eyes, it too from the last days at home. Her youngest brother was adamant: he had to have a bicycle—all his friends, even the poorest, had bicycles. All his mother's pleas were in vain. She had no money. And what she had was not enough. Their father needed medicines. Tzili's seventeen-year-old brother shouted so loudly in the shop that strangers came in to quiet him. The mother wept with rage. And the older sister, who did not leave her books for a moment, shrieked: because of her family she would fail her exams. Tzili now remembered with great clarity her sister's white hand waving despairingly, as if she were drowning.

The day passed slowly, and visions of food no longer troubled her. She saw what was before her eyes: a thin forest and the golden calm of summer. All she had endured in the past days lost its terror.

She was borne forward unthinkingly on a stream of light. Even when she washed her face in the river she felt no strangeness. As if it had always been her habit to do so.

And while she was standing there a rustle went through the field. At first she thought it was the rustle of the leaves, but she immediately realized her mistake: her nose picked up the scent of a man. Before she had time to recover she saw, right next to her, a man sitting on a little hillock.

"Who's there?" said the man, without raising his voice.

"Me," said Tzili, her usual reply to this question.

"Who do you belong to?" he asked, in the village way.

When she did not answer right away, the man raised his head and added: "What are you doing here?"

When she saw that the man was blind, she relaxed and said: "I came to see if the corn was ready for the harvesting." She had often heard these words spoken in the shop. Since the same sentence, with slight variations, was repeated every season, it had become part of her memory.

"The corn came up nicely this year," said the blind man, stroking his jacket. "Am I mistaken?"

"No father, you're not mistaken."

"How high is it?"

"As high as a man, or even higher."

"The rains were plentiful," said the blind man, and licked his lips.

His blind face went blank and he fell silent.

"What time is it?"

"Noon, father."

He was wearing a coarse linen jacket and he was barefoot. He sat at his ease. The years of labor were evident in his sturdy shoulders. Now he was looking for a word to say, but the word evaded him. He licked his lips.

"You're Maria's daughter, aren't you?" he said and chuckled.

"Yes," said Tzili, lowering her voice.

"So we're not strangers."

Maria's name was a household word throughout the district. She had many daughters, all bastards. Because they were all good-looking, like their mother, nobody harmed them. Young and old alike availed themselves of their favors. Even the Jews who came for the summer holidays. In Tzili's house Maria's name was never spoken directly.

A number of years before, Tzili's older brother had gotten one of Maria's daughters into trouble. Maria herself had appeared in the shop and created a scene. For days, the family had consulted in whispers, and in the end they had been obliged to hand over a tidy sum. The mother, worn out with work, had refused to forgive her son. She found frequent occasions to refer to his crime. Tzili had not, of course, grasped the details of the

15

affair, but she sensed that it was something dark and sordid, not to be spoken of directly. Later on, their mother forgave her brother, because he began to study and also to excel.

"Sit down," said the blind man. "What's your hurry?"

She approached and seated herself wordlessly by his side. She was used to the blind. They would congregate outside the shop and sit there for hours at a time. Every now and then her mother would emerge and offer them a loaf of bread, and they would munch it noisily. Mostly they would sit in silence, but sometimes they would grow irritable and begin to quarrel. Her father would go out to restore order. Tzili would sit and watch them for hours. Their mute, upraised faces reminded her of people praying.

The blind man seemed to rouse himself. He groped for his satchel, took out a pear and said: "Here, take it."

Tzili took it and immediately sank her teeth into the fruit.

"I have some smoked meat too—will you have some?"

"I will."

He held the thick sandwich out in his big hand. Tzili looked at the big pale hand and took the sandwich. "Maria's daughters are all good-looking girls," he said and snickered. Now that he had

16

straightened the upper half of his body he looked very strong. Even his white hands. "I don't like eating alone. Eating alone depresses me," he confessed. He chewed calmly and carefully, as blind men will, as if they were suspicious even of the food they put in their mouths.

As he ate he said: "They're killing the Jews. The pests. Let them go to America." But he didn't seem particularly concerned. He was more concerned with the coming harvest.

"Why are you so silent?" he said suddenly.

"What's there to say?"

"Maria's daughters are a cunning lot."

Tzili did not yet know that the notorious name of Maria would be her shield from danger. All her senses were concentrated on the thick sandwich the blind man had given her.

Once Maria had been a customer at the shop. She was a handsome, well-dressed woman and she used city words. They said that Maria had a soft spot for Jews, which did not add to her reputation. Her daughters too had inherited this fondness. And when the Jewish vacationers appeared, Maria would have a taste of what it meant to be indulged.

Tzili now remembered nothing but the heavy scent Maria left behind her in the shop. She liked breathing in this scent.

The blind man said casually: "Maria's daughters

love the Jews, may God forgive them." And he snickered to himself again. Then he sat there quietly, as if he were a cow chewing the cud.

Now there was no sound but for the birds and the rustling of the leaves, and they too seemed muted. The blind man abandoned his full face to the sun and seemed about to fall asleep.

Suddenly he asked: "Is there anyone in the field?"

"No."

"And where did you come from?" The full face smiled.

"From the village square."

"And there's no one in the field?" he asked again, as if he wanted to hear the sound of his own voice.

"No one."

Upon hearing Tzili's reply he reached out and put his hand on her shoulder. Tzili's shoulder slumped under the weight of his hand.

"Why are you so skinny?" said the blind man, apparently encountering her narrow shoulder bones. "How old are you?"

"Thirteen."

"And so skinny." He clutched her with his other hand, too, the one he had been leaning on.

Tzili's body recoiled from the violence of the peasant's embrace, and he threw her onto the ground with no more ado.

A scream escaped her lips.

The blind man, apparently taken aback by this reaction, hurried to stop her mouth but his hand missed its aim and fell onto her neck. Her body writhed under the blind man's heavy hands.

"Quiet! What's the matter with you?" He tried to quiet her as if she were a restless animal. Tzili choked. She tried to wriggle out from under the weight.

"What has your mother been feeding you to make you choke like that?"

The blind man loosened his grip, apparently under the impression that Tzili was too stunned to move. With a swift, agile movement she slipped out of his hands.

"Where are you?" he said, spreading out his hands.

Tzili retreated on her hands and knees.

"Where are you?" He groped on the ground. And when there was no reply, he started waving his hands in the air and cursing. His voice, which had sounded soft a moment before, grew hoarse and angry.

For some reason Tzili did not run away. She crawled on all fours to the field. Evening fell and she curled up. The blind man's strong hands were still imprinted on her shoulders, but the pain faded as the darkness deepened.

Later the blind man's son came to take him home. As soon as he heard his son approaching, the blind man began to curse. The son said that one of the shafts had broken on the way and he had had to go back to the village to get another cart. The father was not convinced by this story and he said: "Why couldn't you walk?"

"Sorry, father, I didn't think of it. I didn't have the sense."

"But for the girls you've got sense enough."

"What girls, father?" said the son innocently.

"God damn your soul," said the blind man and spat.

4

By now Tzili's memories of home were blurred. They've all gone, she said blankly to herself. The little food she ate appeased her hunger. She was tired. A kind of hollowness, without even the shadow of a thought, plunged her into a deep sleep.

But her body had no rest that night. It seethed. Painful sensations woke her from time to time. What's happening to me? she asked herself, not without resentment. She feared her body, as if something alien had taken possession of it.

When she woke and rose to her feet it was still night. She felt her feet, and when she found nothing wrong with them she was reassured. She sat and listened attentively to her body. It was a cloudless and windless night. Above the bowed tops of the corn a dull flame gleamed. From below, the stalks looked like tall trees. She was astonished by the stillness.

And while she stood there listening she felt a liquid oozing from her body. She felt her belly, it was tight but dry. Her muscles throbbed rhythmically. "What's happening to me?" she said.

When dawn broke she saw that her dress was stained with a number of bright spots of blood. She lifted up her dress. There were a couple of spots on the ground too. "I'm going to die." The words escaped her lips.

A number of years before, her oldest sister had cut her finger on a kitchen knife. And by the time the male nurse came, the floor was covered with dark blood stains. When he finally arrived, he clapped his hands to his head in horror. And ever since they had spoken about Blanca's weak, wounded finger in solicitous tones.

"I'm going to die," she said, and all at once she rose to her feet. The sudden movement alarmed her even more. A chill ran down her spine and she shivered. The thought that soon she would be lying dead became more concrete to her than her own feet. She began to whimper like an animal. She knew that she must not scream, but fear made her reckless. "Mother, mother!" she wailed. She went on screaming for a long time. Her voice grew weaker and weaker and she fell to the ground with her arms spread out, as she imagined her body would lie in death.

When she had composed herself a little, she saw her sister sitting at the table. In the last year she had tortured herself with algebra. They had to bring a tutor from the neighboring town. The tutor turned out to be a harsh, strict man and Blanca was terrified of him. She wept, but no one paid any attention to her tears. The father too, from his sick bed, demanded the impossible of her. And she did it too. Although she did not complete the paper and obtained a low mark, she did not fail. Now Tzili saw her sister as she had never seen her before, struggling with both hands against the Angel of Death.

And as the light rose higher in the sky, Tzili heard the trudge of approaching feet. One of the blind man's daughters was leading her father to his place. He was grumbling. Cursing his wife and daughters. The girl did not reply. Tzili listened intently to the footsteps. When they reached his place on the hillock the girl said: "With your permission, father, I'll go back to the pasture now."

"Go!" He dismissed her, but immediately changed his mind and added: "That's the way you honor your father."

"What shall I do, father?" Her voice trembled.

"Tell your father the latest news in the village."

"They chased the Jews away and they killed them too."

"All of them?" he asked, with a dry kind of curiosity.

"Yes, father."

"And their houses? What happened to their houses?"

"The peasants are looting them," she said, lowering her voice as if she were repeating some scandalous piece of gossip.

"What do you say? Maybe you can find me a winter coat."

"I'll look for one, father."

"Don't forget."

"I won't forget."

Tzili took in this exchange, but not its terrible meaning. She was no longer afraid. She knew that the blind man would not move from his place.

5

Hours of silence came. Her oppression lifted. And after her weeping she felt a sense of release. "It's better now," she whispered, to banish the remnants of the fear still congealed inside her. She lay flat on her back. The late summer sunlight warmed her body from top to toe. The last words left her and the old hunger that had troubled her the day before came back.

When night fell she bandaged her loins with her shawl, and without thinking about where she was going she walked on. The night was clear, and delicate drops of light sparkled on the broad cornfields. The bandage pressing against her felt good, and she walked on. She came across a stream and bent down to cup the water in her hands and drink. Only now did she realize how thirsty she was. She sat calmly and watched the running water. The sights of home dissolved in the cool air. Her fear shrank. From time to time brief words or syllables escaped her lips, but they were only the sighs that come after long weeping.

She slept and woke and slept again and saw her old teacher. The look in his eye was neither kindly nor benign, but appraising, the way he looked at her when she was reading from the prayer book. It was a dispassionate, slightly mocking look. Strange, she tried to explain something to him but the words were muted in her mouth. In the end she succeeded in saying: I am setting out on a long journey. Give me your blessing, teacher. But she didn't really say it, she only imagined saying it. Her intention made no impression on the old man, as if it were just one more of her many mistakes.

Afterward she wandered in the outskirts of the forest. Her food was meager: a few wild cherries, apples, and various kinds of sour little fruits which quenched her thirst. The hunger for bread left her. From time to time she went down to the river and dipped her feet in the water. The cold water brought back memories of the winter, her sick father groaning and asking for another blanket. But these were only fleeting sensations. Day by day her body was detaching itself from home. The wound was fresh but not unhealthy. The seeds of oblivion had already been sown. She did not wash her body. She was afraid of removing the shawl from her loins. The sour smell grew worse.

"You must wash yourself," a voice whispered.

"I'm afraid."

"You must wash yourself," the voice repeated.

In the afternoon, without taking off her dress,

she stepped into the river. The water seeped into her until she felt it burn. And immediately drops of blood rose to the surface of the water and surrounded her. She gazed at them in astonishment. Afterward she lay on the ground.

The water was good for her, but not the fruit. In these early days she did not yet know how to distinguish between red and red, between black and black. She plucked whatever came to hand, blackberries and raspberries, strawberries and cherries. In the evening she had severe pain in her stomach and diarrhea. Her slender legs could not stand up to the pain and they gave way beneath her. "God, God." The words escaped her lips. Her voice disappeared into the lofty greenness. If she had had the strength, she would have crawled into the village and given herself up.

"What are you doing here?"

She was suddenly startled by a peasant's voice.

"I'm ill."

"Who do you belong to?"

"Maria."

The peasant stared at her in disgust, pursed his mouth, and turned away without another word.

6

Autumn was already at its height, and in the evenings the horizon was blue with cold. Tzili would find shelter for the night in deserted barns and stables. From time to time she would approach a farmhouse and ask for a piece of bread. Her clothes gave off a bad, moldy smell and her face was covered with a rash of little pimples.

She did not know how repulsive she looked. She roamed the outskirts of the forest and the peasants who crossed her path averted their eyes. When she approached farmhouses to beg for bread the housewives would chase her away as if she were a mangy dog. "Here's Maria's daughter," she would hear them say. Her ugly existence became a byword and a cautionary tale in the mouths of the local peasants, but the passing days were kind to her, molding her in secret, at first deadening and then quickening her with new life. The sick blood poured out of her. She learned to walk barefoot, to bathe in the icy water, to tell the edible berries from the poisonous ones, to climb the trees. The sun worked wonders with her. The visions of the night gradually left her. She saw only what was in

29

front of her eyes, a tree, a puddle, the autumn leaves changing color.

For hours she would sit and gaze at the empty fields sinking slowly into grayness. In the orchards the leaves turned red. Her life seemed to fall away from her, she coiled in on herself like a cocoon. And at night she fell unconscious onto the straw.

One day she came across a hut on the fringes of the forest. Autumn was drawing to a close. It rained and hailed incessantly, and the frost ate into her bones. But she was no longer afraid of anyone, not even the wild dogs.

A woman opened the door and said: "Who are you?"

"Maria's daughter," said Tzili.

"Maria's daughter! Why are you standing there? Come inside!"

The woman seemed thunderstruck. "Maria's daughter, barefoot in this frost! Take off your clothes. I'll give you a gown."

Tzili took off her mildewed clothes and put on the gown. It was a fancy city gown, flowered and soaked in perfume. After many months of wandering, she had a roof over her head.

"Your mother and I were young together once, in the city. Fate must have brought you to my door."

Tzili looked at her from close up: a woman no longer young, with frizzy hair and prominent cheekbones.

"And what is your mother doing now?"

Tzili hesitated a moment and said: "She's at home."

"My name is Katerina," said the woman. "If you see your mother tell her you saw Katerina. She'll be very glad to hear it. We had a lot of good times together in the city, especially with the Jews."

Tzili trembled.

"The Jews are great lovers. Ours aren't a patch on them, I can tell you that—but we were fools then, we came back to the village to look for husbands. We were young and afraid of our fathers. Jewish lovers are worth their weight in gold. Let me give you some soup," said Katerina and hurried off to fetch a bowl of soup.

After many days of wandering, loneliness, and cold, she took in the hot liquid like a healing balm.

Katerina poured herself a drink and immediately embarked on reminiscences of her bygone days in the city, when she and Maria had queened it with the Jews, at first as chambermaids and later as mistresses. Her voice was full of longing.

"The Jews are gentle. The Jews are generous and kind. They know how to treat a woman properly. Not like our men, who don't know anything except how to beat us up." In the course of the years she had learned a little Yiddish, and she still remembered a few words—the word *dafka*, for instance.

31

Tzili felt drawn into the charmed circle of Katerina's memories. "Thank you," she said.

"You don't have to thank me, girl," scolded Katerina. "Your mother and I were good friends once. We sat in the same cafés together, made love to the same man."

Katerina poured herself drink after drink. Her high cheekbones stuck out and her eyes peered into the distance with a birdlike sharpness. Suddenly she said: "The Jews, damn them, know how to give a woman what she needs. What does a woman need, after all? A little kindness, money, a box of chocolates every now and then, a bed to lie on. What more does a woman need? And what have I got now? You can see for yourself.

"Your mother and I were fools, stupid fools. What's there to be afraid of? I'm not afraid of hell. My late mother never stopped nagging me: Katerina, why don't you get married? All the other girls are getting married. And I like a fool listened to her. I'll never forgive her. And you." She turned to Tzili with a piercing look. "You don't get married, you hear me? And don't bring any little bastards into the world either. Only the Jews, only the Jews—they're the only ones who'll take you out to cafés, to restaurants, to the cinema. They'll always take you to a clean hotel, only the Jews."

Tzili no longer took in the words. The warmth and the scented gown cradled her: her head dropped and she fell asleep.

7

From the first day Tzili knew what was expected
of her. She swept the floor and washed the dishes,
she hurried to peel the potatoes. No work was too
arduous for her. The months out of doors seemed
to have taught her what it meant to serve others.
She never left a job half done and she never got
mixed up. And whenever it stopped raining she
would take the skinny old cow out to graze.

Katerina lay in her bed wrapped in goat skins,
coughing and sipping tea and vodka by turn. From
time to time she rose and went to stand by the
window. It was a poor house with a dilapidated
stable beside it. And in the yard: a few pieces of
wood, a gaping fence, and a neglected vegetable
patch. These were the houses outside the village
borders, where the lepers and the lunatics, the
horse thieves and the prostitutes lived. For genera-
tions one had replaced the other here, without re-
pairing the houses or cultivating the plots. The
passing seasons would knead such places in their
hands until they could not be told apart from
abandoned forest clearings.

In the evening the softness would come back to her voice and she would speak again of the days in the city when she and Maria walked the streets together. What was left of all that now? She was here and they were there. In the city a thousand lights shone—and here she was surrounded by mud, madmen and lepers.

Sometimes she put on one of her old dresses, made up her face, stood by the window, and announced: "Tomorrow I'm leaving. I'm sick of this. I'm only forty. A woman of forty isn't ready for the rubbish dump yet. The Jews will take me as I am. They love me."

Of course, these were hallucinations. Nobody came to take her away. Her cough gave her no rest, and every now and then she would wake the sleeping Tzili and command her: "Make me some tea. I'm dying." At night, when a fit of coughing seized her, her face grew bitter and malign, and no one escaped the rough edge of her tongue, not even the Jews.

Once in a while an old customer appeared and breathed new life into the hut. Katerina would get dressed, make up her face, and douse herself with perfume. She liked the robust peasants, who clutched her round the waist and crushed her body to them. Her old voice would come back to her, very feminine. All of a sudden she would be transformed, laughing and joking, reminiscing about times gone by. And she would reprimand Tzili too, and instruct her: "That's not the way to offer a man a drink. A man likes his vodka first, bread later." Or: "Don't cut the sausage so thin."

But such evenings were few and far between. Katerina would wrap herself in blankets and whimper in a sick voice: "I'm cold. Why don't you make the fire properly? The wood's wet. This wetness is driving me out of my mind."

Tzili learned that Katerina was a bold, hot-tempered woman. Knives and axes had no fears for her. At the sight of an unsheathed knife all her beauty burst forth. With drunks she was gentle, speaking to them in a tender and maternal voice.

Although their houses were far apart, Katerina was at daggers drawn with her neighbors. Once a day the leper would emerge from his house and curse Katerina, yelling at the top of his voice. And when he started walking toward her door, Katerina would rush out to meet him like a mad-dened dog. He was a big peasant, his body pink all over from the disease.

Winter came, and snow. Tzili went far into the forest to gather firewood. When she came back in the evening with a bundle of twigs on her shoul-ders bigger than she was, Katerina was still not satisfied. She would grumble: "I'm cold. Why didn't you bring thicker branches? You're spoiled. You need a good hiding. I took you in like a mother and you're shirking your work. You're like your mother. She only looked out for herself. I'm going to give you a good beating."

Of Katerina's plans for her Tzili had no inkling. Her life was one of labor, oblivion, and uncomprehending delight. She delighted in the hut, the faded feminine objects, and the scents that frequently filled the air. She even delighted in the emaciated cow.

From time to time Katerina gave her significant looks: "Your breasts are growing. But you're still too skinny. You should eat more potatoes. How old are you? At your age I was already on the streets." Or sometimes in a maternal voice: "Why don't you comb your hair? People are coming and your hair's not combed."

Winter deepened and Katerina's cough never left her for an instant. She drank vodka and boiling-hot tea, but the cough would not go away. From night to night it grew harsher. She would wake Tzili up and scold her: "Why don't you bring me a glass of tea? Can't you hear me coughing?" Tzili would tear herself out of her sleep and hasten to get Katerina a glass of tea.

It was a long winter and Katerina never stopped grumbling and cursing her sisters, her father, and all the seekers of her favors who had devoured her body. Her face grew haggard. She could no longer stand on her feet. There were no more visitors. The only ones who still came were drunk or crazy.

At first she tried to pretend, but now it was no longer possible to hide her illness. The men fled from the house. Katerina accompanied their flight with curses. But the worst of her rage she spent on Tzili. From time to time she threw a plate or a pot at her. Tzili absorbed the blows in silence. Once Katerina said to her: "At your age I was already keeping my father."

8

Spring came and Katerina felt better. Tzili made up a bed for her outside the door. Now too she kept up a constant stream of abuse, but to Tzili she spoke mildly: "Why don't you go and wash yourself? There's a mirror in the house. Go and comb your hair." And once she even offered her one of her scented creams. "A girl of your age should perfume her neck."

Tzili worked without a break from morning to night. She ate whatever she could lay her hands on: bread, milk, and vegetables from the garden. Her day was full to overflowing. And at night she fell onto her bed like a sack.

No one came to ask for Katerina's favors any more and her money ran out. Even the male nurse, who pulled out two of her teeth, failed to collect his due. Katerina would stand slumped in the doorway.

One evening she asked Tzili: "Have you ever been to bed with a man?"

"No." Tzili shuddered.

"And don't you feel the need? At your age," said Katerina, with almost maternal tenderness, "I had already known many men. I was even married."

"Did you have any children?" asked Tzili.

"I did, but I gave them away when they were babies."

Tzili asked no more. Katerina's face was angry and bitter. She realized that she shouldn't have asked.

Summer came and there was no end to Katerina's complaints. She would speak of her youth, of her lovers, of the city and of money. Now she hardened her heart toward her Jewish lovers too and abused them roundly. The accusations poured out of her in a vindictive stream, scrambled up with fantasies and wishes. Every now and then she would get up and hurl a plate across the room, and the walls would shake with the clatter and the curses. Tzili's movements grew more and more confined, and the old fear came back to her.

From time to time Katerina would berate her: "At your age I was already keeping my father, and you . . ."

"What do you want me to do, mother?"

"Do you have to ask? I didn't have to ask my father. I went to the city and sent him money every month. A daughter has to look after her parents. I let those guzzlers devour my body."

Tzili's heart was full of foreboding. She guessed

that something bad was going to happen, but she
didn't know what. Her happiest hours were the
ones she spent in the meadows grazing the cow.
The air and light kneaded her limbs with a firm
and gentle touch. From time to time she would
take off her clothes and bathe in the river.

Katerina watched her with an eagle eye: "Your
health is improving every day and I'm being eaten
up with illness." Her back was very bent, and
without her front teeth her face had a ghoulish,
nightmare look.

One evening an old client of Katerina's came to
call, a burly middle-aged peasant. Katerina was
lying in bed.

"What's the matter with you?" he asked in surprise.

"I'm resting. Can't a woman rest?"

"I just wanted to say hello," he said, retreating
to the door.

"Why not stay a while and have a drink?"

"I've already had more than enough."

"Just one little drink."

"Thanks. I just dropped in to say hello."

Suddenly she raised herself on her elbows,
smiled and said: "Why don't you take the little
lass to bed? You won't be sorry."

The peasant turned his head with a dull, slow
movement, like an animal, and an embarrassed
smile appeared on his lips.

"She may be small but she's got plenty of flesh

on her bones." Katerina coaxed him. "You can take my word for it."

Tzili was standing in the scullery. The words were quite clear. They sent a shiver down her spine.

"Come here," commanded Katerina. "Show him your thighs."

Tzili stood still.

"Pick up your dress," commanded Katerina.

Tzili picked up her dress.

"You see, I wasn't lying to you."

The peasant dropped his eyes. He examined Tzili's legs. "She's too young," he said.

"Don't be a fool."

Tzili stood holding her dress fearfully in her hands.

"I'll come on Sunday," said the peasant.

"She's got breasts already, can't you see?"

"I'll come on Sunday," repeated the peasant.

"Go then. You're a fool. Any other man would jump at the chance."

"I don't feel like it today. I'll come on Sunday."

But he lingered in the doorway, measuring the little girl with his eyes, and for a moment he seemed about to drag her into the scullery. In the end he recovered himself and repeated: "I'll come on Sunday."

"You fool," said Katerina with an offended air, as if she had offered him a tasty dish and he had refused to eat it. And to Tzili she said: "Don't stand there like a lump of wood."

Tzili dropped her dress.

For a moment longer Katerina surveyed the peasant with her bloodshot eyes. Then she picked up a wooden plate and threw it. The plate hit Tzili and she screamed. "What are you screaming about? At your age I was already keeping my father."

The peasant hesitated no longer. He picked up his heels and ran.

Now Katerina gave her tongue free rein, abusing and cursing everyone, especially Maria. Tzili's fears were concentrated on the sharp knife lying next to the bed. The knife sailed through the air and hit the door. Tzili fled.

9

The night was full and starless. Tzili walked along the paths she now knew by heart. For some reason she kept close to the river. On either side, the cornfields stretched, broad and dark. "I'll go on," she said, without knowing what she was saying.

She had learned many things during the past year: how to launder clothes, wash dishes, offer a man a drink, collect firewood, and pasture a cow, but above all she had learned the virtues of the wind and the water. She knew the north wind and the cold river water. They had kneaded her from within. She had grown taller and her arms had grown strong. The further she walked from Katerina's hut the more closely she felt her presence. As if she were still standing in the scullery. She felt no resentment toward her.

"I'll go on," she said, but her legs refused to move.

She remembered the long, cozy nights at Katerina's. Katerina lying in bed and weaving fantasies about her youth in the city, parties and lovers. Her face calm and a smile on her lips. When she spoke about the Jews her smile narrowed and grew more modest, as if she were revealing some great secret. It seemed then as if she acquiesced in everything, even in the disease devouring her body. Such was life.

Sometimes too she would speak of her beliefs, her fear of God and his Messiah, and at these moments a strange light seemed to touch her face. Her mother and father she could not forgive. And once she even said: "Pardon me for not being able to forgive you."

Tzili felt affection even for the old, used objects Katerina had collected over the years. Gilt powder boxes, bottles of eau de cologne, crumpled silk petticoats and dozens of lipsticks—these objects held an intimate kind of magic.

And she remembered too: "Have you ever been to bed with a man?"

"No."

"And don't you feel the need?"

Katerina's face grew cunning and wanton.

And on one of the last days Katerina asked: "You won't desert me?"

"No," promised Tzili.

"Swear by our Lord Saviour."

"I swear by our Lord Saviour."

Of the extent to which she had been changed by the months with Katerina, Tzili was unaware. Her feet had thickened and she now walked surely

over the hard ground. And she had learned something else too: there were men and there were
women and between them there was an eternal
enmity. Women could not survive save by cunning.

Sometimes she said to herself: I'll go back to
Katerina. She'll forgive me. But when she turned
around her legs froze. It was not the knife itself she
feared but the glitter of the blade.

Summer was at its height, and there was no rain.
She lived on the fruit growing wild on the river
banks. Sometimes she approached a farmhouse.

"Who are you?"

"Maria's daughter."

Maria's reputation had reached even these remote farmhouses. At the sound of her name, a look
of loathing appeared on the faces of the farmers'
wives. Sometimes they said in astonishment:
"You're Maria's daughter!" The farmers themselves were less severe: in their youth they had
availed themselves freely of Maria's favors, and in
later years too they had occasionally climbed into
her bed.

And one day, as she stood in a field, the old
memory came back to confront her: her father lying on his sickbed, the sound of his sighs rending
the air, her mother in the shop struggling with the
violent peasants. Blanca as always, under the
shadow of the impending examinations, a pile of
books and papers on her table. And in the middle

of the panic, the bustle, and the hysteria, the clear sound of her father's voice: "Where's Tzili?"

"Here I am."

"Come here. What mark did you get in the arithmetic test?"

"I failed, father."

"You failed again."

"This time Blanca helped me."

"And it didn't do any good. What will become of you?"

"I don't know."

"You must try harder."

Tzili shuddered at the clear vision that came to her in the middle of the field. For a moment she stood looking around her, and then she picked up her feet and began to run. Her panic-stricken flight blurred the vision and she fell spread-eagled onto the ground. The field stretched yellow-gray around her without a soul in sight.

"Katerina," she said, "I'm coming back to you." As soon as the words were out of her mouth she saw the burly peasant in front of her, examining her thighs as she lifted up her skirt. Now she was no longer afraid of him. She was afraid of the ancient sights pressing themselves upon her with a harsh kind of clarity.

10

In the autumn she found shelter with an old couple. They lived in a poor hut far from everything.

"Who are you?" asked the peasant.

"Maria's daughter."

"That whore," said his wife. "I don't want her daughter in the house."

"She'll help us," said the man.

"No bastard is going to bring us salvation," grumbled the wife.

"Quiet, woman." He cut her short.

And thus Tzili found a shelter. Unlike Katerina's place, there were no luxuries here. The hut was composed of one long room containing a stove, a rough wooden table, and two benches. In the corner, a couple of stools. And above the stools a Madonna carved in oak, as simple as the work of a child.

It was a long, gray autumn, and on the monotonous plains everything seemed made of mud and fog. Even the people seemed to be made of the same substance: rough and violent, their tongue that of the pitchfork and cattle prod. The wife would wake her while it was still dark and push her outside with grunts: go milk the cows, go take them to the meadow.

The long hours in the meadows were her own. Her imagination did not soar but the little she possessed warmed her like soft, pure wool. Katerina, of course. In this gray place her former life with Katerina seemed full of interest. Here there were only cows, cows and speechlessness. The man and his wife communicated in grunts. If they ran short of milk or wood for the fire, the wife never asked why but brandished the rope as a sign that something was amiss.

Here for the first time she felt the full strength of her arms. At Katerina's they had grown stronger. Now she lifted the pitchfork easily into the air. The columns of her legs too were full of muscles. She ate whatever she could lay her hands on, heartily. But life was not as simple as she imagined. One night she awoke to the touch of a hand on her leg. To her surprise it was the old man. The old woman climbed out of bed after him shouting: "Adulterer!" And he returned chastised to his bed.

This was all the old woman was waiting for. After that she spoke to Tzili like a stray mongrel dog.

It was the middle of winter and the days darkened. The snow piled up in the doorway and barred their way out. Tzili sat for hours in the stable with the cows. She sensed the thin pipes joining her to these dumb worlds. She did not know what one said to cows, but she felt the warmth emanating from their bodies seeping into her. Sometimes she saw her mother in the shop struggling with hooligans. A woman without fear. In this dark stable everything seemed so remote— was more like a previous incarnation than her own life.

Between one darkness and the next the old woman would beat Tzili. The bastard had to be beaten so that she would know who she was and what she had to do to mend her ways. The woman would beat her fervently, as if she were performing some secret religious duty.

When spring comes I'll run away, Tzili would say to herself on her bed at night. Or: Why did I ever leave Katerina? She was good to me. Now she felt a secret affection for Katerina's hut, as if it were not a miserable cottage but an enchanted palace.

Sometimes she would hear her voice saying, "The Jews are weak, but they're gentle too. A Jew would never strike a woman." This mystery seemed to melt into Tzili's body and flood it with sweetness. At times like these her mind would shrink to next to nothing and she would be given over entirely to sensations. When she heard Katerina's voice she would curl up and listen as if to music.

But the old man could not rest, and every now

and then he would dart out of bed and try to reach her. And once, in his avidity, he bit her leg, but the old woman was too quick for him and dragged him off before he could go any further. "Adulterer!" she cried.

Sometimes he would put on an expression of injured innocence and say: "What harm have I done?"

"Your evil thoughts are driving you out of your mind."

"What have I done?"

"You can still ask!"

"I swear to you . . ." The old man would try to justify himself.

"Don't swear. You'll roast in hell!"

"Me?"

"You, you rascal."

The winter stretched out long and cold, and the grayness changed from one shade to another. There was nowhere to hide. It seemed that the whole universe was about to sink beneath the weight of the black snow. Once the old woman asked her: "How long is it since you saw your mother?"

"Many years."

"It was from her that you learned your wicked ways. Why are you silent? You can tell us. We know your mother only too well. Her and all her scandals. Even I had to watch my old man day and night. Not that it did me any good. Men are born adulterers. They'd find a way to cheat on their wives in hell itself."

Toward the end of winter the old woman lost control of herself. She beat Tzili indiscriminately. "If I don't make her mend her ways, who will?" She beat her devoutly with a wet rope so that the strokes would leave their mark on her back. Tzili screamed with pain, but her screams did not help her. The old woman beat her with extraordinary strength. And once, when the old man tried to intervene, she said: "You'd better shut up or I'll beat you too. You old lecher. God will thank me for it." And the old man, who usually gave back as good as he got, kept quiet. As if he had heard a warning voice from on high.

11

When the snow began to thaw she fled. The old woman guessed that she was about to escape and kept muttering to herself: "As long as she's here I'm going to teach her a lesson she'll never forget. Who knows what she's still capable of?"

Now Tzili was like a prisoner freed from chains. She ran. The heads of the mountains were still capped with snow, but in the black valleys below, the rivers flowed loud and torrential as waterfalls.

Her body was bruised and swollen. In the last days the old woman had whipped her mercilessly. She had whipped her as if it were her solemn duty to do so, until in the end Tzili too felt that she was only getting what she deserved.

But for the mud she would have walked by the riverside. She liked walking on the banks of the river. For some reason she believed that nothing bad would happen to her next to the water, but she was obliged to walk across the bare mountainside, washed by the melted snow. The valleys were full of mud.

She came to the edge of a forest. The fields

spreading below it steamed in the sun. She sat down and fell asleep. When she woke the sun was on the other side of the horizon, low and cold.

She tried to remember. She no longer remembered anything. The long winter had annihilated even the little memory she possessed. Only her feet sensed the earth as they walked. She knew this piece of ground better than her own body. A strange, uncomprehending sorrow suddenly took hold of her.

She took the rags carefully off her feet and then bound them on again. She treated her feet with a curious solemnity. It did not occur to her to ask what would happen when darkness fell. The sun was sinking fast on the horizon. For some reason she remembered that Katerina had once said to her, in a rare moment of peace: "Women are lucky. They don't have to go to war."

Now she felt detached from everyone. She had felt the same thing before, but not in the same way. Sometimes she would imagine that someone was waiting for her, far away on the horizon. And she would feel herself drawn toward it. Now she seemed to understand instinctively that there was no point going on.

As she sat staring into space, a sudden dread descended on her. What is it? she said and rose to her feet. There was no sound but for the gurgle of the water. On the leafless trees in the distance a blue light flickered.

It occurred to her that this was her punishment. The old woman had said that many punishments were in store for her. "There's no salvation for bastards!" she would shriek.

"What have I done wrong?" Tzili once asked uncautiously.

"You were born in sin," said the old woman. "A woman born in sin has to be cleansed, she has to be purified."

"How is that done?" asked Tzili meekly.

"I'll help you," said the old woman.

That night she found shelter in an abandoned shed. It was cold and her body was sore, but she was content, like a lost animal whose neck has been freed from its yoke at last. She slept for hours on the damp straw. And in her dreams she saw Katerina, not the sick Katerina but the young Katerina. She was wearing a transparent dress, sitting by a dressing table, and powdering her face.

12

When she woke it was daylight. Scented vapors rose from the fields. And while she was sitting there a man seemed to come floating up from the depths of the earth. For a moment they measured each other with their eyes. She saw immediately: he was not a peasant. His city suit was faded and his face exhausted.

"Who are you?" he asked in the local dialect. His voice was weak but clear.

"Me?" she asked, startled.

"Where are you from?"

"The village."

This reply confused him. He turned his head slowly to see if anyone was there. There was no one. She smelled the stale odor of his mildewed clothes.

"And what are you doing here?"

She raised herself slightly on her hands and said: "Nothing."

The man made a gesture with his hand as if he was about to turn his back on her. But then he said: "And when are you going back there?"

"Me?"

Now it appeared that the conversation was over. But the man was not satisfied. He stroked his coat. He seemed about forty and his hands were a grayish white, like the hands of someone who had not known the shelter of a man-made roof for a long time.

Tzili rose to her feet. The man's appearance revolted her, but it did not frighten her. His soft flabbiness.

"Haven't you got any bread?" he asked.

"No."

"And no sausage either?"

"No."

"A pity. I would have given you money for them," he said and turned to go. But he changed his mind and said in a clear voice: "Haven't you got any parents?"

This question seemed to startle her. She took a step backward and said in a weak voice: "No."

Her reply appeared to excite the stranger, and he said with a kind of eagerness: "What do you say?" The trace of a crooked smile appeared on his gray-white face.

"So you're one of us."

There was something repulsive about his smile. Her body shrank and she recoiled. As if some loathsome reptile had crossed her path. "Tell me," he pressed her, standing his ground. "You're one of us, aren't you?"

For a moment she wanted to say no and run away, but her legs refused to move.

"So you're one of us," he said and took a few steps toward her. "Don't be afraid. My name's Mark. What's yours?"

He took off his hat, as if he wished to indicate with this gesture not only respect but also submission. His bald head was no different from his face, a pale gray.

"How long have you been here?"

Tzili couldn't open her mouth.

"I've lost everyone. I'd made up my mind to die tonight." Even this sentence, which was spoken with great emotion, did not move her. She stood frozen, as if she were caught up in an incomprehensible nightmare. "And you, where are you from? Have you been wandering for long?" he continued rapidly, in Tzili's mother tongue, a mixture of German and Yiddish, and with the very same accent.

"My name is Tzili," said Tzili.

The man seemed overcome. He sank onto his knees and said: "I'm glad. I'm very glad. Come with me. I have a little bread left."

Evening fell. The fruit trees on the hillside glowed with light. In the forest it was already dark.

"I've been here a month already," said the man, composing himself. "And in all that time I haven't seen a soul. What about you? Do you know anybody?" He spoke quickly, swallowing his words, getting out everything he had stored up in the long, cold days alone. She did not understand much, but one thing she understood: in all the countryside around them there were no Jews left.

"And your parents?" he asked.

Tzili shuddered. "I don't know, I don't know. Why do you ask?"

The stranger fell silent and asked no more.

In his hideout, it transpired, he had some crusts of bread, a few potatoes, and even a little vodka.

"Here," he said, and offered her a piece of bread.

Tzili took the bread and immediately sank her teeth into it.

The stranger looked at her for a long time, and a crooked smile spread over his face. He sat cross-legged on the ground. After a while he said: "I couldn't believe at first that you were Jewish. What did you do to change yourself?"

"Nothing."

"Nothing, what do you say? I will never be able to change. I'm too old to change, and to tell the truth I don't even know if I want to."

Later on he asked: "Why don't you say anything?" Tzili shivered. She was no longer accustomed to the old words, the words from home. She had never possessed an abundance of words, and the months she had spent in the company of the old peasants had cut them off at the roots. This stranger, who had brought the smell of home back

to her senses, agitated her more than he frightened
her.

When it grew dark he lit a fire. He explained: the
entire area was surrounded by swamps. And now
with the thawing of the snow it would be inacces-
sible to their enemies. It was a good thing that the
winter was over. There was a practical note now
in his voice. The suffering seemed to have vanished from his face, giving way to a businesslike
expression. There was no anger or wonder in it.

13

When she woke there was light in the sky and the man was still sitting opposite her, in the same position. "You fell asleep," he said. He rose to his feet and his whole body was exposed: medium height, a worn-out face, and a crumpled suit, very faded at the knees. A few spots of grease. Swollen pockets.

"Ever since I escaped from the camp I haven't been able to sleep. I'm afraid of falling asleep. Are you afraid too?"

"No," said Tzili simply.

"I envy you."

The signs of spring were everywhere. Rivulets of melted snow wound their way down the slopes, dragging gray lumps of ice with them. There was not a soul to be seen, only the sound of the water growing louder and louder until it deafened them with its roar.

He looked at her and said: "If you hadn't told me, I'd never have guessed that you were Jewish. How did you do it?"

"I don't know. I didn't do anything."

"If I don't change they'll get me in the end. Nothing will save me. They won't let anyone escape. I once saw them with my own eyes hunting down a little Jewish child."

"And do they kill everyone?" Tzili asked.

"What do you think?" he said in an unpleasant tone of voice.

His face suddenly lost all its softness and a dry, bitter expression came over his lips. Her uncautious question had apparently angered him.

"And where were you all the time?" he demanded.

"With Katerina."

"A peasant woman?"

"Yes."

He dropped his head and muttered to himself. Apparently in anger, and also perhaps regret. His cheekbones projected, pulling the skin tight.

"And what did you do there?" He went on interrogating her.

"I worked."

"And did she know that you were Jewish?"

"No."

"Strange."

In the afternoon he grew restless and agitated. He ran from tree to tree, beating his head with his fists and reproaching himself: "Why did I run away? Why did I have to run away? I abandoned them all and ran away. God will never forgive me."

Tzili saw him in his despair and said nothing. The old words which had begun to stir in her retreated even further. In the end she said, for some reason: "Why are you crying?"

"I'm not crying. I'm angry with myself."

"Why?"

"Because I'm a criminal."

Tzili was sorry for asking and she said: "Forgive me."

"There's nothing to forgive."

Later on he told her. He had escaped and left his wife and two children behind in the camp. He had tried to drag them too through the narrow aperture he had dug with his bare hands, but they were afraid. She was, his wife.

And while he was talking it began to rain. They found a shelter under the branches. The man forgot his despair for a moment and spread a tattered blanket over the branches. The rain stopped.

"And did you too leave everyone behind?" he asked.

Tzili said nothing.

"Why don't you tell me?"

"Tell you what?"

"How you got away?"

"My parents left me behind to look after the house. They promised to come back. I waited for them."

"And ever since then you've been wandering?"

For some reason he tore off a lump of bread and offered her a piece.

She gnawed it without a word.

"The bread should be heated up. It's wet."

"It doesn't matter."

"Don't you suffer from pains in your stomach?"

"No."

"I suffer terribly from pains in my stomach."

The rain stopped and a blue-green light floated above the horizon. The gurgling of the water had given way to a steady flow. The man washed his face in the rivulet and said: "How good it is. Why don't you wash your face in the water too?"

Tzili took a handful of water and washed her face.

They sat silently by the little stream. Tzili felt that her life had led her to a new destination, it too unknown. The closeness of the man did not excite her, but his questions upset her. Now that he had stopped asking she felt better.

Suddenly he raised his eyes from the water and said: "Why don't you go down to the village and bring us something to eat? We have nothing to eat. The little we had is gone."

"All right, I'll go," she said.

"And you won't forget to come back?"

"I won't forget," she said, blushing.

Immediately he corrected himself and said: "You can buy whatever you want, it doesn't matter, as long as it's something to fill our bellies. I'd go myself, and willingly, but I'd be found out. It's a pity I haven't got any other clothes. You understand."

"I understand," said Tzili submissively.

"I'd go myself if I could," he said again, in a tone which was at once ingratiating and calculating. "You, how shall I put it, you've changed, you've changed for the better. Nobody would ever suspect you. You say your r's exactly like they do. Where do you get it all from?"

"I don't know."

Now there was something frightening in his appearance. As if he had risen from his despair another man, terrifyingly practical.

14

Early in the morning she set out. He stood watching her receding figure for a long time. Once again she was by herself. She knew that the stranger had done something to her, but what? She walked for hours, looking for ways around the melted snow, and in the end she found an open path, paved with stones.

A woman was standing next to one of the huts, and Tzili addressed her in the country dialect: "Have you any bread?"

"What will you give me for it?"

"Money."

"Show me."

Tzili showed her.

"And how much will I give you for it?"

"Two loaves."

The old peasant woman muttered a curse, went inside, and emerged immediately with two loaves in her hands. The transaction was over in a moment.

"Who do you belong to?" she remembered to ask.

"To Maria."

"Maria? *Tfu*." The woman spat. "Get out of my sight."

Tzili clasped the bread in both hands. The bread was still warm, and it was only after she had walked for some distance that the tears gushed out of her eyes. For the first time in many days she saw the face of her mother, a face no longer young. Worn with work and suffering. Her feet froze on the ground, but as in days gone by she knew that she must not stand still, and she continued on her way.

The trees were putting out leaves. Tzili jumped over the puddles without getting wet. She knew the way and weaved between the paths, taking shortcuts and making detours like a creature native to the place. She walked very quickly and arrived before evening fell. Mark was sitting in his place. His tired, hungry eyes had a dull, indifferent look.

"I brought bread," she said.

Mark roused himself: "I thought you were lost." He fell on the bread and tore it to shreds with his teeth, without offering any to Tzili. She observed him for a moment: his eyes seemed to have come alive and all his senses concentrated on chewing.

"Won't you have some too?" he said when he was finished eating.

Tzili stretched out her hand and took a piece of

bread. She wasn't hungry. The long walk had tired her into a stupor. Her tears too had dried up. She sat without moving.

Mark passed his right hand over his mouth and said: "A cigarette, if only I had a cigarette."

Tzili made no response.

He went on: "Without cigarettes there's no point in living." Then he dug his nails into the ground and began singing a strange song. Tzili remembered the melody but she couldn't understand the words. Gradually his voice lost its lilt and the song trailed off into a mutter.

The evening was cold and Mark lit a fire. During the long days of his stay here he had learned to make fire from two pieces of flint and a thread of wool which he plucked from his coat. Tzili marveled momentarily at his dexterity. The agitation faded from his face and he asked in a practical tone of voice: "How did you get the bread? Fresh bread?"

Tzili answered him shortly.

"And they didn't suspect you?"

For a long time they sat by the little fire, which gave off a pleasant warmth.

"Why are you so silent?"

Tzili hung her head, and an involuntary smile curved her lips.

The craving for cigarettes did not leave him. The fresh bread had given him back his taste for life, but he lost it again immediately. For hours he sat nibbling blades of grass, chewing them up and spitting them to one side. He had a tense, bitter look. From time to time he cursed himself for being a slave to his addiction. Tzili was worn out and she fell asleep where she sat.

15

When she woke she kept her eyes closed. She felt Mark's eyes on her. She lay without moving. The fire had not gone out, which meant that Mark had not slept all night.

When she finally opened her eyes it was already morning. Mark asked: "Did you sleep?" The sun rose in the sky and the horizons opened out one after the other until the misty plains were revealed in the distance. Here and there they could see a peasant ploughing.

"It's a good place," said Mark. "You can see a long way from here." The agitation had faded from his face, and a kind of complacency that did not suit him had taken its place. Tzili imagined she could see in him one of the Jewish salesmen who used to drop into her mother's shop. Mark asked her: "Did you go to school?"

"Yes."

"A Jewish school?"

"No. There wasn't one. I studied Judaism with an old teacher. The Pentateuch and prayers."

"Funny," he said, "it sounds so far away. As if it never happened. And do you still remember anything?"

"Hear, O Israel."

"And do you recite it?"

"No," she said and hung her head.

"In my family we weren't observant any more," said Mark in a whisper. "Was your family religious?"

"No, I don't think so."

"You said they brought you a teacher of religion."

"It was only for me, because I didn't do well at school. My brothers and sisters were all good at school. They were going to take external examinations."

"Strange," said Mark.

"I had trouble learning."

"What does it matter now?" said Mark. "We're all doomed anyway."

Tzili did not understand the word but she sensed that it held something bad.

After a pause Mark said: "You've changed very nicely, you've done it very cleverly. I can't imagine a change like that taking place in me. Even the forests won't change me now."

"Why?" asked Tzili.

"Because everything about me gives me away— my appearance, from top to toe, my nose, my accent, the way I eat, sit, sleep, everything. Even though I've never had anything to do with what's called Jewish tradition. My late father used to call himself a free man. He was fond of that phrase, I remember, but here in this place I've discovered, looking at the peasants ploughing in the valley, their serenity, that I myself—I won't be able to change anymore. I'm a coward. All the Jews are cowards and I'm no different from them. You understand."

Tzili understood nothing of this outburst, but she felt the pain pouring out of the words and she said: "What do you want to do?"

"What do I want to do? I want to go down to the village and buy myself a packet of tobacco. That's all I want. I have no greater desire. I'm a nervous man and without cigarettes I'm an insect, less than an insect, I'm nothing."

"I'll buy it for you."

"Thank you," said Mark, ashamed. "Forgive me. I have no more money. I'll give you a coat. That's good, isn't it?"

"Yes, that's good," said Tzili. "That's very good."

In the tent of branches he had a haversack full of things. He spread them out now on the ground to dry. His clothes, his wife's and children's clothes. He spread them out slowly, like a merchant displaying his wares on the counter.

Tzili shuddered at the sight of the little garments spotted with food stains. Mark spread them out without any order and they steamed and gave off a stench of mildew and sour-sweet. "We must dry them," said Mark in a businesslike tone. "Otherwise they'll rot." He added: "I'll give you my coat. It's a good coat, pure wool. I bought it a year ago. I hope you'll be able to get me some cigarettes for it. Without cigarettes to smoke I get very nervous."

Strange, his nervousness was not apparent now. He stood next to the steaming clothes, turning them over one by one, as if they were pieces of meat on a fire. Tzili too did not take her eyes off the stained children's clothes shrinking in the sun.

Toward evening he gathered the clothes up carefully and folded them. The coat intended for selling he put aside. "For this, I hope, we'll be able to get some tobacco. It's a good coat, almost new," he muttered to himself.

That night Mark did not light a fire. He sat and sucked soft little twigs. Chewing the twigs seemed to blunt his craving for cigarettes. Tzili sat not far from him, staring into the darkness.

"I wanted to study medicine," Mark recalled, "but my parents didn't have the money to send me to Vienna. I sat for external matriculation exams and my marks weren't anything to write home about, only average. And then I married very young, too young I'd say. Of course, nothing came of my plans to study. A pity."

"What's your wife's name?" asked Tzili.

"Why do you ask?" said Mark in surprise.

"No reason."

"Blanca."

"How strange," said Tzili. "My sister's name is Blanca too."

Mark rose to his feet. Tzili's remark had abruptly stopped the flow of his memories. He put his hands in his trouser pocket, stuck out his chest, and said: "You must go to sleep. Tomorrow you have a long walk in front of you."

The strangeness of his voice frightened Tzili and she immediately got up and went to lie down on the pile of leaves.

16

She slept deeply, without feeling the wind. When she woke a mug of hot herb tea was waiting for her.

"I couldn't sleep," he said.

"Why can't you sleep?"

"I can't fall asleep without a cigarette."

Tzili put the coat into a sack and rose to her feet.

Mark sat in his place next to the fire. His dull eyes were bloodshot from lack of sleep. For some reason he touched the sack and said: "It's a good coat, almost new."

"I'll look after it," said Tzili without thinking, and set off.

I'll bring him cigarettes, he'll be happy if I bring him cigarettes. This thought immediately strengthened her legs. The summer was in full glory, and in the distant, yellow fields she could see the farmers cutting corn. She crossed the mountainside and when she came to the river she picked up her dress and waded across it. Light burst from every direction, bright and clear. She approached the plots of cultivated land without fear, as if she had known them all her life. With every step she felt the looseness of the fertile soil.

"Have you any tobacco?" she asked a peasant woman standing at the doorway of her hut.

"And what will you give me in exchange?"

"I have a coat," said Tzili and held it up with both hands.

"Where did you steal it?"

"I didn't steal it. I got it as a present."

Upon hearing this reply an old crone emerged from the hut and announced in a loud voice: "Leave the whore's little bastard alone." But the younger woman, who liked the look of the coat, said: "And what else do you want for it?"

"Bread and sausage."

Tzili knew how to bargain. And after an exchange of arguments, curses, and accusations, and after the coat had been turned inside out and felt all over, they agreed on two loaves of bread, two joints of meat, and a bundle of tobacco leaves.

"You'll catch it if the owner comes and demands his coat back. We'll kill you," the old crone said threateningly.

Tzili put the bread, meat, and tobacco into her sack and turned to go without saying a word. The old crone showed no signs of satisfaction at the transaction, but the young woman made no attempt to hide her delight in the city coat.

On the way back Tzili sat and paddled in the

water. The sun shone and silence rose from the
forest. She sat for an hour without moving from
her place and in the end she said to herself: Mark
is sad because he has no cigarettes. When he has
cigarettes he'll be happy. This thought brought her
to her feet and she started to run, taking shortcuts
wherever she could.

Toward evening she arrived. Mark bowed his
head as if she had brought him news of some great
honor, an honor of which he was not unworthy.
He took the bundle of tobacco leaves, stroking and
sniffing them. Before long he had a cigarette rolled
from newspaper. An awkward joy flooded him. In
the camp people would fight over a cigarette stub
more than over a piece of bread. He spoke of the
camp now as if he were about to return to it.

That evening he lit a fire again. They ate and
drank herb tea. Mark found a few dry logs and
they burned steadily and gave off a pleasant
warmth. The wind dropped too, and seemed gentler than before, the shadows it brought from the
forest less menacing. Mark was apparently affected by these small changes. Without any warning he suddenly burst into tears.

"What's wrong?"

"I remembered."

"What?"

"Everything that's happened to me in the past
year."

Tzili rose to her feet. She wanted to say something but the words would not come. In the end she said: "I'll bring you more tobacco."

"Thank you," he said. "I sit here eating and smoking and they're all over there. Who knows where they are by now." His gray face seemed to grow grayer, a yellow stain spread over his forehead.

"They'll all come back," said Tzili, without knowing what she was saying.

These words calmed him immediately. He asked about the way and the village, and how she had obtained the food and the tobacco, and in general what the peasants were saying.

"They don't say anything," said Tzili quietly.

"And they didn't say anything about the Jews?"

"No."

For a few minutes he sat without moving, wrapped up in himself. His dull, bloodshot eyes slowly closed. And suddenly he dropped to the ground and fell asleep.

17

Every week she went down to the plains to renew
their supplies. She was quiet, like a person doing
what had to be done without unnecessary words.
She would bathe in the river, and when she returned her body gave off a smell of cool water.

She would tell him about her adventures on the
plains: a drunken peasant woman had tried to hit
her, a peasant had set his dog on her, a passerby
had tried to rob her of the clothes she had taken to
barter. She spoke simply, as if she were recounting
everyday experiences.

And because the weather was fine, and the rains
scattered, they would sit for hours by the fire eating, drinking herb tea, listening to the forest and
hardly speaking. Mark stopped speaking of the
camp and its horrors. He spoke now about the advantages of this high, remote place. And once he
said: "The air here is very fresh. Can you feel how
fresh it is?" He pronounced the word "fresh" very
distinctly, with a secret happiness. Sometimes he
used words that Tzili did not understand.

Once Tzili asked what the words "out of this world" meant.

"Don't you understand?"

"No."

"It's very simple: out of this world—out of the ordinary, very nice."

"From God?" she puzzled.

"Not necessarily."

But it wasn't always like this. Sometimes a suppressed rage welled up in him. "What happened to you? Why are you so late?" When he saw the supplies, he recovered his spirits. In the end he would ask her pardon. She, for her part, was no longer afraid of him.

Day by day he changed. He would sit for hours looking at the wild flowers growing in all the colors of the rainbow. Sometimes he would pluck a flower and whisper: "How lovely, how modest." Even the weeds moved him. And once he said, as if talking to himself: "In Jewish families there's never any time. Everyone's in a hurry, everyone's in a panic. What for?" There was a kind of music in his voice, a melancholy music.

The days went by one after the other and nothing happened to arouse their suspicions. On the contrary, the silence deepened. The corn was cut in one field after the other and the fruit was gathered in the orchards, and Mark, for some reason, decided to dig a bunker, in case of trouble.

This thought came to him suddenly one afternoon, and he immediately set out to survey the terrain. Straight away he found a suitable place, next to a little mound covered with a tangle of thorns. In his haversack he had a simple kitchen knife. This domestic article, dull with use, fired the desire for activity in him. He set to work to make a spade. The hard, concentrated work changed his face; he stopped talking, as if he had found a purpose for his transitory life, a purpose in which he drowned himself completely.

Every week Tzili went down to the plains and brought back not only bread and sausages but also vodka, in exchange for the clothes which Mark gave her with an abstracted expression on his face. His outbursts did not cease, but they were only momentary flare-ups, few and far between. Activity, on the whole, made him agreeable.

Once he said to her: "My late father's love for the German language knew no bounds. He had a special fondness for irregular verbs. He knew them all. And with me he was very strict about the correct pronunciation. The German lessons with my father were like a nightmare. I always got mixed up and in his fanaticism he never overlooked my mistakes. He made me write them down over and over again. My mother knew German well but not perfectly, and my father would lose his temper and correct her in front of other people. A mistake in grammar would drive him out of his mind. In the provinces people are more fanatical about the German language than in the city."

"What are the provinces?" asked Tzili.

"Don't you know? Places without gymnasiums, without theaters." Suddenly he burst out laughing. "If my father knew what the products of his culture were up to now he would say, 'Impossible, impossible.'"

"Why impossible?" said Tzili.

"Because it's a word he used a lot."

After many days of slow, stubborn carving, Mark had a spade, a strong spade. The carved instrument brightened his eyes, and he couldn't stop touching it. He was in good spirits and he told her stories about all the peculiar tutors his father hired to teach him mathematics and Latin. Young Jewish vagabonds, for the most part, who had not completed their university degrees, who ended up by getting some girl, usually not Jewish, into trouble, and had to be sent packing in a hurry. Mark told these stories slowly, imitating his teachers' gestures and describing their various weaknesses, their fondness for alcohol, and so on. This language was easier for Tzili to understand. Sometimes she would ask him questions and he would reply in detail.

And then he started digging. He worked for hours at a stretch. Every now and then it started raining and the digging was disrupted. Mark would grow angry, but his anger did not last long. The backbreaking work gave him the look of a simple laborer. Tzili stopped asking questions and Mark stopped telling stories.

After a week of work the bunker was ready, dug firmly into the earth. And it was just what was needed for the cold autumn season, a shelter for the cold nights. Mark was sure that the Germans would never reach them, but it was better to be careful, just in case. Tzili noticed that Mark often used the word *careful* now. It was a word he had hardly ever used before.

He put the finishing touches to the bunker without excitement. A quiet happiness spread over his face and hands. Now she saw that his cheeks were tanned and his arms, which had seemed so weak and flabby, were full and firm. He looked like a laboring man who knew how to enjoy his labors.

What will happen when we've sold all the clothes? the thought crossed Tzili's mind. This thought did not appear to trouble Mark. He was so pleased with the bunker, he kept repeating: "It's a good bunker, a comfortable bunker. It will stand up well to the rain."

18

After this the days grew cold and cloudy and Mark drank a lot of vodka. The tan faded suddenly from his face. He would sit silently, and sometimes he would talk to himself, as if Tzili weren't there. On her return from the plains he would ask: "What did you bring?" If she had brought vodka he would say nothing. If she hadn't he would say: "Why didn't you bring vodka?"

At night the words would well up in him and come out in long, clumsy, half-swallowed sentences. Tzili could not understand, but she sensed: Mark was now living in another world, a world which was full of people. Day after day he sat and drank. His face grew lean. There was a kind of strength in this leanness. His days became confused with his nights. Sometimes he would fall asleep in the middle of the day and sometimes he would sit up until late at night. Once he turned to her in the middle of the night and said: "What are you doing here?"

"Nothing."

"Why don't you go down to the village and bring supplies? Our supplies are running out."

"It's night."

"In that case," he said, "we'll wait for the dawn."

He's sad, he's drunk, she would murmur to herself. If I bring him tobacco and vodka he'll feel better. She no longer dared to return without vodka. Sometimes she would sleep in the forest because she was afraid to come back without vodka.

At that time Mark said many strange and confused things. Tzili would sit at a distance and watch him. Alien hands seemed to be clutching at him and kneading him. Sometimes he would lie in his vomit like a hired hand on a drunken spree. His old face, the face of a healthy working man, was wiped away.

And once in his drunkenness he cried: "If only I'd studied medicine I wouldn't be here. I'd be in America." In his haversack, it transpired, were a couple of books which he had once used to prepare for the entrance exams to Vienna University. And once, when it seemed to her that he was calmer, he suddenly burst out in a loud cry: "Commerce has driven the Jews out of their minds. You can cheat people for one year, even for one hundred years, but not for two thousand years!" In his drunkenness he would shout, make speeches, tear sentences to shreds and piece them together again.

Tzili sensed that he was struggling with people who were far away and strangers to her, but nevertheless—she was afraid. His lean cheeks were full of strength. On her return from the plains she would hear his voice from a long way off, rending the silence.

And again, just when she thought that his agitation had died down, he fell on her without any warning: "Why didn't you learn French?"

"We didn't learn French at school, we learned German."

"Barbarous. Why didn't they teach you French? And it's not as if you know German either. What you speak is jargon. It drives me out of my mind. There's no culture without language. If only people learned languages at school the world would be a different place. Do you promise me that you'll learn French?"

"I promise."

Afterward it began to rain and Mark dragged himself to the bunker. A rough wind was blowing. Mark's words went on echoing in the air for a long time. And Tzili, without knowing what she was doing, went up to the bunker and called softly: "It's me, Tzili. Don't worry. Tomorrow I'll bring you vodka and sausage."

19

After this the autumn weather grew finer and a cold, clear sun shone on their temporary shelter. Mark's troubled spirit seemed to lighten too and he stopped cursing. He didn't stop drinking, but his drinking no longer put him in a rage. Now he would often say: "There was something I wanted to say, but it's slipped my mind." A weak smile would break through the clouds, darkening his face. Far-off, forgotten things continued to trouble him, but not in the same shocking way. Now he would speak softly of the need to study languages, acquire a liberal profession, escape from the provinces, but he no longer scolded Tzili.

He would speak of the approaching winter as a frontier beyond which lay life and hope. And Tzili sensed that Mark was now absorbed in listening to himself. Every now and then he would conclude aloud: "There's still hope. There's still hope."

And once he questioned her about her religious studies. Tzili's life at home now felt so remote and scattered that it didn't seem to belong to her. On the way to the plains she would wonder about Maria, whose name she had so unthinkingly adopted. The more she thought about her, the clearer her features grew. A tall, proud woman, she gave her body to anyone who wanted it, but not without getting a good price. And when her daughters grew up, they too adopted their mother's gestures, they too were bold.

She didn't tell him about Maria, just as she didn't tell him about Katerina. Her femininity blossomed within her, blind and sweet. Outwardly too she changed. The pimples didn't disappear from her face, but her limbs were full of strength. She walked easily, even when she had a heavy sack to carry.

"How old are you?" Mark had once asked her in the days of his drunkenness. Afterward he didn't ask again. Now he would beg her pardon for his drunken behavior; his face recovered its former mildness. Tzili's happiness knew no bounds. Mark had recovered and he would never shout at her again. For some reason she believed that the new drink, which the peasants called slivovitz, was responsible for this change.

It seemed to Tzili that the happy days of the summer were about to return, but she was wrong. Mark now craved a woman. This secret he was keeping even from himself. He would urge Tzili to go down to the plains even before it was necessary. Her blooming presence was driving him wild.

And while Tzili was busy pondering ways and means of getting hold of the new, calming drink, Mark suddenly said: "I love you."

Tzili's mouth fell open. His voice was familiar, but very different. She was surprised, but not altogether. The last few nights had been cold and they had both slept in the bunker. They had sat together until late at night, with a warm, dark intimacy between them.

Mark stretched out his arms and clasped her round the waist. Tzili's body shrank from his hands. "You don't love me," he mumbled. The tighter he held her, the more her body shrank. But he was determined, and he slid her dress up with nimble fingers. "No," she managed to murmur. But it was already too late.

Afterward he sat by her side and stroked her body. Strange words came tumbling out of his mouth. For some reason he began talking again about the advantages of the place, the beautiful marshes, the forests, and the fresh air. The words were external, and they brushed past her naked body like a cold wind.

From now on they stayed in the bunker. The rain poured down, but for the time being they were sheltered against it. Mark drank all the time, but never to excess. His happiness was a drunken happiness, and he wanted to cut it up into little pieces and make it last. From time to time he ventured out to confirm what he already knew—that outside it was cold, dark, and damp.

"Tell me about yourself. Why don't you tell me?" he would press her. The truth was that he only wanted to hear her voice. He showered many words on her during their days together in the bunker. His heart overflowed. Tzili, for her part, accepted her happiness quietly. Secretly she was glad that Mark loved her.

Their supplies ran short. Tzili put off going out from day to day. She liked it in this new darkness. She learned to drink the insidious drug, and the more she drank the more slothful her body became. "I'd go myself, but the peasants would betray me." Mark would excuse himself. And in the meantime the rain and cold hemmed them in. They snuggled up together and their small happiness knew no bounds.

Distant sights, hungry malevolent shadows invaded the bunker in dense crowds. Tzili did not know the bitter, emaciated people. Mark went outside and cut branches with his kitchen knife to block up the openings, hurling curses in all directions. For a moment or two it seemed that he had succeeded in chasing them off. But the harder the rain fell the more bitter the struggle became, and from day to day the shadows prevailed. In vain

Tzili tried to calm him. His happiness was being attacked from every quarter. Tzili too seemed affected by the same secret poison.

"Enough," he announced, "I'm going down."

"No, I'll go," said Tzili.

The dark, rainy plains now drew Mark to them. "I have to go on a tour of inspection," he announced. It was no longer a caprice but a spell. The plains drew him like a magnet.

20

But in the meantime they put off the decision from day to day. They learned to go short and to share this frugality too. He would drink only once a day and smoke only twice, half a cigarette. The slight tremor came back to his fingers, like a man deprived of alcohol. But for the many shadows besieging their temporary shelter, their small happiness would have been complete.

From time to time, when the shadows deepened, he would go outside and shout: "Come inside, please. We have a wonderful bunker. It's a pity we haven't got any food. Otherwise we'd hold a banquet for you." These announcements would calm them, but not for long.

Afterward he said: "There's nothing else for it, we'll have to go down. Death isn't as terrible as it seems. A man, after all, is not an insect. All you have to do is overcome your fear." These words did not encourage Tzili. The dark, muddy plains became more frightening from day to day. Now it seemed that not only the peasants lay in wait for her there but also her father, her mother, and her sisters.

And reality stole upon them unawares. Wetness began to seep through the walls of the bunker. At first only a slight dampness, but later real wetness. Mark worked without a pause to stop up the cracks. The work distracted him from the multitude of shadows lying in wait outside. From time to time he brandished his spade as if he were chasing away a troublesome flock of birds.

One evening, as they were lying in the darkness, snuggling up to each other for warmth, the storm broke in and a torrent of water flooded the bunker. Mark was sure that the multitudes of shadows waiting in the trees to trap him were to blame. He rushed outside, shouting at the top of his voice: "Criminals."

Now they stood next to the trees, looking down at the gray slopes shivering in the rain. And just when it seemed that the steady, penetrating drizzle would never stop, the clouds vanished and a round sun appeared in the sky.

"I knew it," said Mark.

If only Tzili had said, "I'll go down," he might have let her go. Perhaps he would have gone with her. But she didn't say anything. She was afraid of the plains. And since she was silent, Mark said: "I'm going down."

In the meantime they made a little fire and drank herb tea. Mark was very excited. He spoke in lofty, dramatic words about the need to change, to adapt to local conditions, and not to be afraid. Fear corrupts human dignity, he said. The resolution he had had while building the bunker came back to his face. Now he was even more resolute, determined to go down to the plains and not to be afraid.

"Don't go," said Tzili.

"I must go down. Inspection of the terrain has become imperative—if only from the point of view of general security needs. Who knows what the villagers have got up their sleeves? They may be getting ready for a surprise attack. I can't allow them to take us by surprise."

Tzili could not understand what he was talking about, but the lofty, resolute words, which at first had given her a sense of security, began to hurt her, and the more he talked the more they stung. He spoke of reassessment and reappraisal, of diversion and camouflage. Tzili understood none of his many words, but this she understood: he was talking of another world.

"Don't go." She clung to him.

"You have to understand," he said in a gentle voice. "Once you conquer your fear everything looks different. I'm happy now that I've conquered my fear. All my life fear has tortured me shamefully, you understand, shamefully. Now I'm a free man."

Afterward they sat together for a long time. But

although Tzili now said, "I'll go down. They know me, they won't hurt me," Mark had made up his mind: "This time I'm going down." And he went down.

21

Mark receded rapidly and in a few minutes he was gone. She sat still and felt the silence deepening around her. The sky changed color and a shudder passed over the mountainside.

Tzili rose to her feet and went into the bunker. It was dark and warm inside the bunker. The haversack lay to one side. For the past few days Mark had refused to go into the bunker. "A man is not a mole. This lying about is shameful." He used the word *shameful* often, pronouncing it in a foreign accent, apparently German.

The daylight hours crept slowly by, and Tzili concentrated her thoughts on Mark's progress across the mountainside. She imagined him going up and down the same paths that she herself had taken. She saw him pass by the hut where she had bartered a garment for a sausage. She saw it all so clearly that she felt as if she herself were there with him.

In the afternoon she lit a fire and said: "I'll make Mark some herb tea. He likes herb tea."

Mark was late.

"Don't worry, he'll come back," a voice from home said in her ear. But when twilight fell and Mark did not return anxiety began dripping into her soul. She went down to the river and washed the mugs. The cold water banished the anxiety for a moment. For some reason she spread a cloth on the ground.

Darkness fell. The days she had spent with Mark had blunted her fear of the night. Now she was alone again. Mark's voice came to her and she heard: "A man is not an insect. Death isn't as terrible as it seems." Now these words were accompanied by the music of a military band. Like in her childhood, on the Day of Independence, when the army held parades and the bugles played. The military voice gave her back a kind of confidence.

Mark was late.

Now she felt that the domestic smells that had enveloped the place were fading away. Fresh, cold air blew in their place. It occurred to her that if she took the clothes out of the haversack and spread them around, the homely smells would come back to fill the air, and perhaps Mark would sense them. Immediately she took the haversack out of the bunker and spread the clothes on the ground. The brightly colored clothes, all damp and crumpled, gave off a confined, moldy smell.

He's lost, he must be lost. She clung to this sentence like an anchor. She fell to her knees by the clothes. They were children's clothes, small and shrunken with the damp, spotted with food stains and a little torn.

Afterward she turned aside to listen. Apart from an occasional rustle or murmur there was nothing to be heard. From the distant huts scattered between the swamps, isolated barks reached her ears.

After midnight a thin drizzle began to fall and she put the things back into the bunker. This small activity revived an old scene in her memory. She remembered the first days, before the bunker, when she had brought him the tobacco. The way he had rolled the shredded leaves in a piece of newspaper, the way he had recovered his looks, his smile, and the light on his face.

The rain stopped but the wind grew stronger, bending the trees with broad, sweeping movements. Tzili went into the bunker. It was warm and full of the smell of tobacco. She breathed in the smell.

She sat in the dark and for some reason she thought about Mark's wife. Mark seldom spoke of her. Once she had even sensed a note of resentment against her. She imagined her as a tall, thin woman sheltering her children under her coat. Strange, she felt a kind of kinship with her.

22

The next day Mark still did not return. She stood on the edge of the plateau exposed to the wind. The downward slope drew her too. The slope was not steep and it glittered with puddles of water. Now she felt that something had been taken from her, something that belonged to her youth. She covered her face in shame.

For hours she sat and practiced the words, so that she would be ready for him when he came. "Where were you Mark? I was very worried. Here is some herb tea for you. You must be thirsty." She did not prepare many words, and the few she did prepare, she repeated over and over again in a voice which had a formal ring in her ears. Repeating the words put her to sleep. She would wake up in alarm and go to the bunker. The walls of the bunker had collapsed, the flimsy roof had caved in, and the floor was covered by a spreading gray puddle. There was an alien spirit in it, but it was the only place she could go to. Everywhere else was even more alien.

The days dragged out long and heavy. Tzili did

not stir. And once a voice burst out from within her: "Mark." The voice slid down the mountainside, echoing as it went. No one answered.

Overnight the winds changed and the winter winds came, thin and sharp as knives. The fire burned but it did not warm her. Low, dark clouds covered the somber sky. She prayed often. This was the prayer which she repeated over and over: "God, bring Mark back. If you bring Mark back to me, I'll go down to the plains and I won't be lazy."

How many days had Mark been gone? At first she kept track, but then she lost count. Sometimes she saw Mark struggling with the peasants and hurling pointed sticks at them, like the ones he had made for the walls of the bunker. Sometimes he looked tired and crushed. Like the first time she had seen him, pale and gray. Man is not an insect, she remembered and made an effort to get up and stand erect.

For days she had had nothing to eat. Here and there she still found a few withered wild apples, but for the most part she now lived off roots. The roots were sweet and juicy. "I'll go on," she said, but she didn't move. For hours she sat and gazed at the mountainside sloping down to the plains, the two marshes, the shelter, and the haversack. Sometimes she took out the clothes and spread them on the ground, but Mark did not respond to her call.

The moment she decided to leave she would

imagine that she heard footsteps approaching. A little longer, she would say to herself. Death is not as terrible as it seems.

Sometimes the cold would envelop her in sweetness. She would close her eyes and curl up tightly and wait for a hand to come and take her away. But none came. Winter winds tore across the hillside, cruel and cutting. "I'll go on," she said, and lifted the haversack onto her shoulders. The haversack was soaked through and heavy, with every step she felt that the burden was too heavy to bear.

"Did you see a man pass by?" she asked a peasant woman standing at the doorway of her hut.

"There's no man here. They've all been conscripted. Who do you belong to?"

"Maria."

"Which Maria?"

And when she did not reply the peasant woman understood which Maria she meant, snickered aloud, and said: "Be off with you, wretch! Get out of my sight."

One by one Tzili gave the little garments away in exchange for bread. "If I meet Mark I'll tell him that I was hungry. He won't be angry." The haversack on her back grew more burdensome from day to day but she didn't take it off. The damp warmth stuck to her back. She went from tree to tree. She believed that next to one of the trees she would find him.

23

It began to snow and she was obliged to look for work. The long tramp had weakened her. Overnight she lost her freedom and became a serf.

At this time the Germans were on the retreat, but here it was the middle of winter and the snow fell without a break. The peasants drove her mercilessly. She cleaned the cow shed, milked the cows, peeled potatoes, washed dishes, brought firewood from the forest. At night the peasant's wife would mutter: "You know who your mother is. You must pay for your sins. Your mother has corrupted whole villages. If you follow in her footsteps I'll beat you black and blue."

Sometimes she went out at night and lay down in the snow. For some reason the snow refused to absorb her. She would return to her sufferings, meek and submissive. One evening on her way back from the forest she heard a voice. "Tzili," called the voice.

"I'm Tzili," said Tzili. "Who are you?"

"I'm Mark," said the voice. "Have you forgotten me?"

"No," said Tzili, frightened. "I'm waiting for you. Where are you?"

"Not far," said the voice, "but I can't come out of hiding. Death is not as terrible as it seems. All you have to do is conquer your fear."

She woke up. Her feet were frozen.

From then on Mark appeared often. He would surprise her at every turn, especially his voice. It seemed to her that he was hovering nearby, unchanged but thinner and unable to emerge from his hiding place. And once she heard quite clearly: "Don't be afraid. The transition is easy in the end." These apparitions filled her with a kind of warmth. And at night, when the stick or the rope fell on her back, she would say to herself, "Never mind. Mark will come to rescue you in the spring."

And in the middle of the hard, grim winter she sensed that her belly had changed and was slightly swollen. At first it seemed an insignificant change. But it did not take long for her to understand: Mark was inside her. This discovery frightened her. She remembered the time when her sister Yetty fell in love with a young officer from Moravia, and everyone became angry with her. Not because she had fallen in love with a gentile but because the intimate relations between them were likely to get her into trouble. And indeed, in the end it came out that the officer was an immoral drunkard, and but for the fact that his regiment was transferred the affair would certainly have ended badly. It remained as a wound in her sister's heart, and at home it came up among other unfortunate affairs in whispers, in veiled words. And Tzili, it transpired, although she was very young at the time, had known how to put the pieces together and make a picture, albeit incomplete.

There was no more possibility of doubt: she was pregnant. The peasant woman for whom she slaved soon noticed that something was amiss. "Pregnant," she hissed. "I knew what you were the minute I set eyes on you."

Tzili herself, when the first fear had passed, suddenly felt a new strength in her body. She worked till late at night, no work was too hard for them to burden her with, but she did not weaken. She drew strength from the air, from the fresh milk, and from the hope that one day she would be able to tell Mark that she was bearing his child. The complications, of course, were beyond her grasp.

And in the meantime the peasant woman beat her constantly. She was old but strong, and she beat Tzili religiously. Not in anger but in righteousness. Ever since her discovery that Tzili was pregnant her blows had grown more violent, as if she wanted to tear the embryo from her belly.

Heaven and hell merged into one. When she went to graze the cow or gather wood in the forest she felt Mark close by her side, even closer than in the days when they had slept together in the bunker. She spoke to him simply, as if she were chatting to a companion while she worked. The work did not stop her from hearing his voice. His words too were clear and simple. "I'll come in the spring," he said. "In the spring the war will end and everyone will return."

Once she dared to ask him: "Won't your wife be angry with me?"

"My wife," said Mark, "is a very forgiving woman."

"As for me," said Tzili, "I love your children as if they were my own."

"In that case," said Mark in a practical tone of voice, "all we have to do is wait for the war to end."

But at night when she returned to the hut reality showed itself in all its nakedness. The peasant's wife beat her as if she were a rebellious animal, in a passion of rage and fury. At first Tzili screamed and bit her lips. Later she stopped screaming. She absorbed the blows with her eyes closed, as if she knew that this was her lot in life.

One night she snatched the rope from the woman and said: "No, you won't. I'm not an animal. I'm a woman." The peasant's wife, apparently startled by Tzili's resolution, stood rooted to the spot, but she immediately recovered, snatched the rope from Tzili's hand, and began to beat her with her fists.

It was the height of winter and there was nowhere to escape to. She worked, and the work strengthened her. The thought that Mark would come for her in the spring was no longer a hope but a certainty.

Once the peasant's wife asked her: "Who made you pregnant?"

"A man."

"What man?"

"A good man."

"And what will you do with the baby when it's born?"

"I'll bring it up."

"And who will provide for you?"

"I'll work, but not for you." The words came out of her mouth directly and quietly.

The peasant's wife ranted and raved.

The next day she said to Tzili: "Take your things and get out of my sight. I never want to see you again."

Tzili took up the haversack and left.

24

Once more she had won her freedom. At that time
the great battlefronts were collapsing, and the first
refugees were groping their way across the broad
fields of snow. Against the vast whiteness they
looked like swarms of insects. Tzili was drawn
toward them as if she realized that her fate was no
different from theirs.

Strange, precisely now, at the hour of her new-
found freedom, Mark stopped speaking to her.
"Where are you and why don't you speak to me?"
she would ask in despair. Nothing stirred in the
silence, and but for her own voice no other voice
was heard.

In one of the bunkers she came across three
men. They were wrapped from top to toe in heavy,
tattered coats. Their bloodshot eyes peeped
through their rags, alert and sardonic.

"Who are you?"

"My name is Tzili."

"So you're one of us. Where have you left everyone?"

"I," said Tzili, "have lost everyone."

"In that case why don't you come with us? What have you got in that haversack?"

"Clothes."

"And haven't you got any bread?" one of them said in an unpleasant voice.

"Who are you?" she asked.

"Can't you see? We're partisans. Haven't you got any bread in that haversack?"

"No I haven't," she said and turned to go.

"Where are you going?"

"I'm going to Mark."

"We know the whole area. There's no one here. You'd better stay with us. We'll keep you amused."

"I," said Tzili opening her coat, "am a pregnant woman."

"Leave the haversack with us. We'll look after it for you."

"The haversack isn't mine. It belongs to Mark. He left it in my care."

"Don't boast. You should learn to be more modest."

"I'm not afraid. Death is not as terrible as it seems."

"Cheeky brat," said the man and rose to his feet. Tzili stared at him.

"Where did you learn that?" said the man, taking a step backward.

Tzili stood still. A strength not hers was in her eyes.

"Go then, bitch," said the man and went back to the bunker.

From then on the snow stretched before her white and empty. Tzili felt a kind of warmth spreading through her. She walked along a row of trees, which now seemed rootless, stuck into the snow like pegs.

From time to time a harassed survivor appeared, asked the way, and disappeared again. Tzili knew that her fate was no different from the survivors, but she kept away from them as if they were brothers who might say: "We told you so."

And while she was walking without knowing where her feet would lead her, the walls of snow began to shudder. It was the month of March and new winds invaded the landscape. On the mountain slopes the first stripes of brown earth appeared. Not long afterward the brown stripes widened.

And suddenly she saw what she had not seen before: the mountain, undistinguished and not particularly lofty, the mountain where she and Mark had spent the summer, and not far from where she was standing the foot of the slope, and next to it the valley leading to Katerina's house. As if the whole world had narrowed down to a piece of land which she could feel with her hands.

She stood for a moment as if she were trying to absorb all these painful places into her body. She herself felt no pain.

And while she was standing there sunk into herself a refugee approached her and he said: "Jewish girl, where are you from?"

"From here."

"And you weren't in the camps?"

"No."

"I lost everyone. What shall I do?"

"In the spring they'll all come back. I'm sure of it."

"How do you know?"

"I'm quite sure. You can believe me." There was strength in her voice. And the man stood rooted to the spot.

"Thank you," he said, as if he had been given a great gift.

"Don't mention it," said Tzili, as she had been taught to say at home.

Without asking for further details, the man vanished as abruptly as he had appeared.

Evening drew near and the last rays of the sun fell golden on the hillside. "I lived here and now I'm leaving," said Tzili, and she felt a slight twinge in her chest. The embryo throbbed gently in her belly. Her vision narrowed even further. Now she could picture to herself the paths lying underneath the carpet of snow. There was no resentment in her heart, only longing, longing for the earth on which she stood. Everything beyond this little corner of the world seemed alien and remote to her.

For days she had not tasted food. She would sit for hours sucking the snow. The melted snow assuaged her hunger. The liquids refreshed her. Now she felt a faint anxiety.

And while she was standing transfixed by what she saw, Mark rose up before her.

"Mark," the word burst from her throat.

Mark seemed surprised. He stood still. And then he asked: "Why are you going to the refugees? Don't you know how bad they are?"

"I was looking for you."

"You won't find me there. I keep as far away as possible from them."

"Where are you?"

"Setting sail."

"Where to?"

All at once a flock of birds rose into the air and crossed the darkening horizon, and Tzili understood that he had only called her in order to take his leave.

She put the haversack down on the snow. Her eyes opened and she said: "My search was in vain." It was her own voice which had come back to her.

"So you're abandoning me to the refugees, those

bad, wicked people." A voice that had been locked up inside her broke out and rose into the air. "I'm asking you a question. Answer me. If you don't want me, tell me. I'm not complaining. I love you anyway. I'll make you herb tea if you like. The mountain is unoccupied. It's waiting for us. There's no one there; we can go back to it. It's a good mountain, you said so yourself. I'll go to the village and bring back supplies, I won't be lazy. You can believe me. Don't you believe me?"

After this she sat for hours next to the haversack. She woke up and fell asleep again, and when she finally rose to her feet brown vapors were already rising from the valleys. Here and there a peasant stretched himself as if after a long sleep. There were no refugees to be seen.

"So you're abandoning me," the old anger flickered up in her again. It wasn't really anger, but only a weak echo of anger. She was with herself as if after a long hunger. She narrowed her eyes and stroked her belly, and then she said to herself: "Mark's probably not allowed to leave, for the time being. Later on, they'll let him go. He's not his own boss, after all."

The snow thawed and the first convoys of refugees poured down the hillsides. Strange, thought Tzili, the war's over and I didn't know. Mark must have known before me; he must be happy now. Suddenly she felt that her life was moving toward some other destination, where the colors were different. She heard the voices of the refugees, and the sound was so familiar that it hurt her.

She thought that she would go to the high mountain where she had first met Mark. She set her steps in that direction but the road was covered with mud and she gave up. Later, she said to herself.

Afterward the commotion died down and the lips of the land could be heard quietly sucking all over the plains. The liquids were being absorbed into the earth.

"Thank you, Maria," said Tzili. "Thanks to you I'm still alive. But for you I would already be in another world. Thanks to you I'm still here. Isn't it strange that thanks to you I'm still here? I'm grateful to you, Maria." Tzili was surprised by the words that came out of her mouth.

She let the memory of Maria flow over her for a moment, and as she did so she saw her figure emerge from the mist and stand solidly before her eyes. A tall, strong woman dressed with simple elegance. When she came into her mother's shop she filled it with the breath of city streets, cafés, and theaters. She never hid her opinions. She would often say that she was fond of the Jews, although not the religious ones. Those she had always hated, but the freethinking Jews who lived in the city were men after her own heart. They knew what civilization meant; they knew how to get the most out of life in the city. Of course, her appearances would always be accompanied by a certain fear, because of her connections with the provincial officials, the tax collectors, the police, and the hospitals. And when her daughters grew up, the circle of her acquaintances was enlarged. Not without scandals, of course.

And when Tzili's brother got one of her daughters into trouble, Maria's tone changed. She threatened them brutally, and in the end she extorted a tidy sum. Tzili remembered this episode too, but she felt no resentment. A proud woman, she concluded to herself.

Katerina, with whom she had spent two whole seasons, had often used this combination of words—"a proud woman." Katerina too, Tzili now remembered with affection.

And while Tzili was standing there in a kind of trance, the refugees streamed toward her in a hungry swarm. She wanted to run for her life, but it was too late. They surrounded her on all sides: "Who are you?"

"I'm from here." At last she found the words.

"And where were you during the war?"

"Here."

"Can't you see?" One of the refugees interrupted. "She's afraid."

"And you weren't in any of the camps?"

"No."

"And no one gave you away?"

"Can't you see?" The same man intervened again. "She doesn't look Jewish. She looks healthy."

"A miracle," said the questioner and turned aside.

The news spread from one to the other but it made no impression on the refugees.

Later on Tzili asked: "Did you see Mark?"

"What's his last name?" asked a woman.

Tzili hung her head. She did not know.

The cold spring sun exposed them like moles. A motley crew of men, women, and children. The cold light showed up their ragged clothes. The convoy turned south and Tzili went with them. No one asked, "Where are you from?" or "Where are you going?" From time to time a supply-laden cart appeared and the people swarmed over it like ants. The familiar words from home now sounded wild and foreign to her. The refugees did not appear contented with anything. They argued, laughed, and fought, and at night they fell to the ground like sacks.

"What am I doing here?" Tzili asked herself. "I prefer the mountains and the rivers. Mark himself told me not to go with them. If I go too far, who knows if I'll ever find him?"

From here she could still see the mountain where Mark had revealed himself to her, illuminated in the cold evening light. Now the bun-

127

ker was ruined and the wind blew through it. Her voice broke with longing. No memory stirred in her, only a thin stream of longing flowing out of her toward the distant mountaintop. The calm of evening fell upon the deserted ranges and she fell asleep.

25

They made their way southward. The peasants
stood by the roadside displaying their wares:
bread, vodka, and smoked meat. But the refugees
walked past without buying or bartering. Suffering
had made them indifferent. But Tzili was hungry.
She sold a garment and received bread and
smoked meat in exchange. "Look," said one of the
survivors, "she's eating."

Now she saw them from close up: thin, speech-
less, and withdrawn. The terror had not yet faded
from their faces.

The sun sank in the sky and the crust of the
earth dried up. The first ploughmen appeared on
the mountainsides next to the plains. There were
no clouds to darken the sky, only the trees, and the
quietness.

They moved slowly through the landscape,
looking around them as they walked. They slept a
lot. Hardly a word was spoken. A kind of secret
veiled their faces. Tzili feared this secret more
than the dark nights in the forest.

A convoy of prisoners was led past in chains. From time to time a soldier fired a shot into the air and the prisoners all bent their heads at once. No one looked at them. The survivors were sunk into themselves.

A man came up to Tzili and asked: "Where are you from?" It wasn't the man himself who asked the question, but something inside him, as in a nightmare.

Tzili felt as if her eyes had been opened. She heard words which she had not heard for years, and they lapped against her ears with their whispers. "If I meet my mother, what will I say to her?" She did not know what everyone else already knew: apart from this handful of survivors, there were no Jews left.

The sun opened out. The people unbuttoned their damp clothes and sprawled on the river bank and slept. The long, damp years of the war steamed out of their moldy bodies. Even at night the smell did not disappear. Only Tzili did not sleep. The way the people slept filled her with wonder. A warm breeze touched them gently in their deep sleep. Are they happy? Tzili asked herself. They slept in a heap, defenseless bodies suddenly abandoned by danger.

The next day too no one woke up. "What do they do in their sleep?" she asked without knowing what she was asking. "I'll go on," she said. "No one will notice my absence. I'll work for the peasants like I did before. If I work hard they'll give me bread. What more do I need?" Her thoughts flowed as of their own accord. All the years of the war, in the forest and on the roads, even when she and Mark were together, she had not thought. Now the thoughts seemed to come floating up to the surface of her mind.

For a moment she thought of getting up and leaving the sleeping people and returning to the mountain where she had first met Mark. The mountain itself had disappeared from view, but she could still see the swamps below it. They shone like two polished mirrors. Her longings were deep and charged with heavy feelings. They drew her like a magnet, but as soon as she rose to her feet she felt that her body had lost its lightness. Not only her belly was swollen but also her legs. The light, strong columns which had borne her like the wind were no longer what they had been.

Now she knew that she would never go back to that enchanted mountain; everything that had happened there would remain buried inside her. She would wander far and wide, but she would never see the mountain again. Her fate would be the fate of these refugees sleeping beside her.

She wanted to weep but the tears remained locked inside her. She sat without moving and felt the sleep of the refugees invading her body. And soon she too was deep in sleep.

26

Their sleep lasted a number of days. From time to time one of them opened his eyes and stretched his arms as if he were trying to wake up. All in vain. He too, like everyone else, was stuck to the ground.

Tzili opened the haversack and spread the clothes out to dry. Two long dresses, a petticoat, children's trousers, the kitchen knife which Mark had used to make the bunker, and two books—this is what was left.

From the size of the garments Tzili understood that Mark's wife was a tall, slender woman and the children were about five years old, thin like their mother. And she noticed too that the dresses buttoned up to the neck, which meant that Mark's wife was from a traditional family. The petticoat was plain, without any flowers. There were two yellow stains on it, apparently from the damp.

She sat looking at the inanimate objects as if she were trying to make them speak. From time to time she stroked them. The silence all around, as in the wake of every war, was profound.

Whenever she felt hunger gnawing at her stomach she would take a garment from the haversack and offer it in exchange for food. At first she had asked Mark to forgive her, although then too, she had not given the matter too much thought. Later she had stopped asking. She was often hungry and she bartered one garment after the other. The haversack had emptied fast, and now this was all that was left.

These things I won't sell, she said to herself, although she knew that the first time she felt hungry she would have to sell them. She would often feel a voracious greed for food, a greed she could not overcome. Mark will understand, she said to herself, it's not my fault.

She sat and listened to the pulsing of the embryo inside her. It floated quietly in her womb, and from time to time it kicked. It's alive, she told herself, and she was glad.

The next day spring burst forth in a profusion of flowers. And the sleepers awoke. It was not an easy awakening. For hours they went on lying, stuck to the ground. Not as many as they had seemed at first—about thirty people all told.

In the afternoon, as the heat of the sun increased, a few of them rose to their feet. In the light of the sun they looked thin and somewhat transparent. Someone approached her and said: "Where are you from?" He spoke in German Jewish. He looked like Mark, only taller and younger.

"From here," said Tzili.

"I don't understand," said the man. "You weren't born here, were you?"

"Yes," said Tzili.

"And what did you speak at home?"

"We tried to speak German."

"That's funny, so did we," said the stranger, opening his eyes wide. "My grandmother and grandfather still spoke Yiddish. I liked the way they talked."

Tzili had never seen her grandfather. This grandfather, her father's father, a rabbi in a remote village in the Carpathian mountains, had lived to a ripe old age and had never forgiven his son for abandoning the faith of his fathers. His name was never mentioned at home. Her mother's parents had died young.

"Where are we going?" the man asked.

"I don't know."

"I have to get there soon. My engineering studies were interrupted in the middle. I've missed enough already. If I don't arrive in time I may be too late to register. A person starts a course of study and all of a sudden a war comes and messes everything up."

"Where were you during the war?" asked Tzili.

"Why do you ask? With everyone else, of course. Can't you see?" he said and stretched out his arm. There was a number there, tattooed in dark blue on his skin. "But I don't want to talk about it. If I start talking about it, I'll never stop. I've made up my mind that from now on I'm starting my life again. And for me that means studying. Completing my studies, to be precise."

This logic astounded Tzili. Now she saw: the man spoke quietly enough, but his right hand waved jerkily as he spoke and fell abruptly to his side, as if it had been cut off in midair.

He added: "I've always been an outstanding student. My average was ninety. And that's no joke. Of course, it made the others jealous. But what of it? I was only doing what I was supposed to do. I like engineering. I've always liked it."

Tzili was enchanted by his eloquence. It was a long time since she had heard such an uninterrupted flow of words. It was the way Blanca and Yetty and her brothers used to talk. Exams, exams always around the corner. Now the words momentarily warmed her frozen memory.

After a pause he said: "There were two exams I didn't take, through no fault of my own. I won't let them get away with it. It wasn't my fault."

"Never mind," said Tzili, for some reason.

"I won't let them get away with it. It wasn't my fault."

And for a moment it seemed that they were sitting, not in an open field in the spring after the war, but in a salon where coffee and cheesecake were being served. The hostess asks: "Who else wants coffee?" A student on vacation speaks of his achievements. Tzili now remembered her own home, her sister Blanca, sulkily hunching her shoulder, her books piled on the table.

The man rose to his feet and said: "I'm not hanging around here. I haven't got any time to waste. These people are sleeping as if time lasts forever."

"They're tired," said Tzili.

"I don't accept that," said the man, with a peculiar gravity. "There's a limit to what a person can afford to miss. I've made up my mind to finish. I'm not going to leave my studies broken off in the middle. I have to get there in time. If I arrive in time I'll be able to register for the second semester."

Tzili asked no more. His eloquence stunned her. And as he spoke, scene after scene of a drama not unfamiliar to her unfolded before her eyes: a race whose demanding pace had not been softened even by the years of war.

He looked around him and said: "I'm going. There's nothing for me to do here."

Tzili remembered that Mark too had stood on the mountainside and announced firmly that he was going. If she had said to him then, "Don't go," perhaps he would not have gone.

"Mark," she said.

The man turned his head and said, "My name isn't Mark. My name's Max, Max Engelbaum. Remember it."

"Don't go," said Tzili.

"Thank you," said the man, "but I haven't any time to waste. I have no intention of spending my time sleeping. And in general, if you understand me, I don't want to spend any more time in the company of these people." He made a funny little half bow, like a clerk rising from his desk, and abruptly said: "Adieu."

Tzili noticed that he walked away the way people had walked toward the railway station in former days, with brisk, purposeful steps which from a distance looked slightly ridiculous.

"Adieu," he called again, as if he were about to step onto the carriage stair.

The awakening lasted a number of days. It was a slow, wordless awakening. The refugees sat on the banks of the river and gazed at the water. The water was very clear now and a kind of radiance shone on its surface. No one went down to bathe. From time to time a word or phrase rose into the air. They were struggling with the coils of their sleep, which were still lying on the ground.

Tzili felt that she had come a very long way. And if she stayed with these people she would go even further away. Where was Mark? Was he too following her, or was he perhaps still waiting, imprisoned in the same place? Perhaps he did not know that the war was over.

And while she was sitting and staring, a woman came up to her and said: "You need milk."

"I have none," said Tzili apologetically.

"You need milk, I said." The woman was no longer young. Her face was haggard and there was a kind of fury in the set of her mouth.

"I'll see to it," said Tzili, in order to appease the woman's wrath.

"Do it straight away. A pregnant woman needs milk. It's as necessary to her as the air she breathes, and you sit here doing nothing."

Tzili said no more. When she did not respond, the woman grew angry and said: "A woman should look after her body. A woman is not an insect. And by the way, where's the bastard who did this to you?"

"His name is Mark," said Tzili softly.

"In that case, let him take care of it."

"He's not here."

"Where is he?"

Tzili sat looking at her without resentment. No one interfered. They were sitting sunk into themselves. The woman turned away and went to sit on the river bank.

That night cool spring winds blew, bringing with them shadows from the mountains. Quiet shadows that clung soundlessly to the trees but that nevertheless caused a commotion. At first people tried to chase them away as if they were birds, but for some reason the shadows clung to the trees and refused to go.

And as if to spite them, the night was very bright, and they could see the shadows clearly, breathing fearfully.

"Go away, leave us alone!" The shouts arose from every side. And when the shadows refused to go, people began to beat them.

The shadows did not react. Their stubborn resistance infuriated the people and they cast off all restraint.

All night long the battle lasted. Bodies and shadows fought each other in silence, violently. The only sound was the thud of their blows.

When day broke the shadows fled.

The survivors were not happy. A kind of sadness darkened their daylight hours. Tzili did not stir from her corner. She too was affected by the sadness. Now she understood what she had not understood before: everything was gone, gone forever. She would remain alone, alone forever. Even the fetus inside her, because it was inside her, would be as lonely as she. No one would ever ask again: "Where were you and what happened to you?" And if someone did ask, she would not reply. She loved Mark now more than ever, but she loved his wife and children too.

The woman who had grown angry with her before on account of the milk now sat wrapped up in herself. A kind of tenderness shone from her eyes, as if she were, not a woman who had lost herself and all she possessed, but a woman with children, whose love for her children was too much for her to bear.

27

Spring was now at its height, its light was everywhere. Some of the people could not bear the silence and left. The rest sat on the ground and played cards. The old madness, buried for years, broke out: cards and gambling. All at once they shook off their damp, rotting rags and put on carefree expressions, laughing and teasing each other. Tzili did not yet know that a new way of life was unconsciously coming into being here.

The holiday atmosphere reminded Tzili of her parents. When she was still small they had spent their summer vacations in a pension on the banks of the Danube. Her parents were short of money, but they had spared no effort in order to be in the company, if only for two weeks, of speakers of correct German. As if to spite them, however, most of the people there spoke Yiddish. This annoyed her father greatly, and he said: "You can't get away from them. They creep in everywhere." Afterward he fell ill, and they stayed at home and spent their money on doctors and medicine.

No one spoke of the war anymore. The card

games devoured their time. A few of them went to buy supplies, but as soon as they got back they joined enthusiastically in the game. Every now and then someone would remember to say: "What will become of us?" But the question was not serious. It was only part of the game. "What's wrong with staying right here? We've got plenty of coffee, cigarettes—we can stay here for the rest of our lives"—someone would nevertheless take the trouble to reply.

Not far from where they sat the troops passed by, a vigorous army liberated from the siege, invading the countryside on fresh young horses. They all admired the Russians, the volunteers and the partisans, but it was not an admiration which entailed a desire for action. "Let the soldiers fight, let them avenge us."

Tzili was with herself and the tiny fetus in her womb. Words which Mark had spoken to her on the mountain rang in her ears. Scenes from the mountain days passed before her eyes like vivid, ritual tableaus. Mark no longer appeared to her. For hours she sat and waited for him to reveal himself. He's dead—the thought flashed through her mind and immediately disappeared.

One evening a few more Jewish survivors appeared, bringing a new commotion. And one of them, a youthful-looking man, spoke of the coming salvation. He spoke of the cleansing of sins, the purification of the soul. He spoke eloquently, in a pleasant voice. His appearance was not ravaged. Thin, but not horrifyingly thin. Some of them recognized him and remembered him from the camp as a quiet young man, working and suffering in silence. They had never imagined that he had so much to say.

Tzili liked the look of him and she drew near to hear him speak. He spoke patiently, imploringly, without raising his voice. As if he were speaking of things that were self-evident. And for a moment it seemed that he was not speaking, but singing.

The people were absorbed in their card game, and the young man's eloquence disturbed them. At first they asked him to leave them alone and go somewhere else. The young man begged their pardon and said that he had only come to tell them what he himself had been told. And if what he had been told was true, he could not be silent.

It was obvious that he was a well-brought-up young man. He spoke politely in a correct German Jewish, and wished no one any harm. But his apologies were to no avail. They ordered him to leave, or at any rate to shut up. The young man seemed about to depart, but something inside him, something compulsive, stopped him, and he stood his ground and went on talking. One of the card players, who had been losing and was in a bad mood, stood up and hit him.

To everyone's surprise, the young man burst out crying.

It was more like wailing than crying. The whole night long he sat and wailed. Through his wailing the history of his life emerged. He was an architect. Like his father and forefathers, he was remote from Jewish affairs, busy trying to set up an independent studio. The war took him completely by surprise. In the camp something had happened to him. His workmate in the forced labor gang, something of a Jewish scholar although not a believer, had taught him a little Bible, Mishna, and the Sayings of the Fathers. After the war he had begun to hear voices, clear, unconfused voices, and one evening the cry had burst from his throat: "Jews repent, return to your Father in Heaven."

From then on he never stopped talking, explaining, and calling on the Jews to repent. And when people refused to listen or hit him, he fell to the ground and wept.

The next day one of the card players found a way to get rid of him. He approached the young man and said to him in his own language, in a whisper: "Why waste your time on these stubborn Jews? Down below, not far from here, there are plenty of survivors, gentle people like you. They're waiting for someone to come and show them the way. You'll do it. You're just the right person. Believe me."

Strange, these words had an immediate effect. He rose to his feet and asked the way, and without another word he set out.

Tzili felt sorry for the young man who had been led astray. She covered her face with her hands. The others too seemed unhappy. They returned to their card playing as if it were not a game, but an urgent duty.

28

After this the weather was fine and mild, without wind or rain. The grass grew thick and wild and the people sat about drinking coffee and playing cards. There were no quarrels, and for a while it seemed as if things would go on like this forever.

From time to time peasant women would appear, spread out their wares on flowered cloths, and offer the survivors apples, smoked meat, and black bread. The survivors bartered clothes for food. Some of them had gold coins too, old watches, and all kinds of trinkets they had kept with them through the years of the war. They gave these things away for food without haggling about their worth.

Tzili too sold a dress. In exchange she received a joint of smoked meat, two loaves of fresh bread, and a piece of cheese. She remembered the woman's anger and asked for milk, but they had no milk. Tzili sat on the ground and ate heartily.

Apart from the card game nobody took any interest in anything. The woman who had scolded

Tzili for not providing herself with milk played avidly. Tzili sat and watched them for hours at a time. Their faces reminded her of people from home, but nevertheless they looked like strangers. Perhaps because of the smell, the wet rot of years which clung to them still.

And while they were all absorbed in their eager game, a sudden fear fell on Tzili. What would she do if they all came back? What would she say, and how would she explain? She would say that she loved Mark. She now feared the questions she would be asked more than she feared the strangers. She curled up and closed her eyes. The fear which came from far away invaded her sleep too. She saw her mother looking at her through a very narrow slit. Her face was blurred but her question was clear: Who was this seducer, who was this Mark?

And Tzili's fears were not in vain. One evening everything exploded. One of the card players, a quiet man with the face of a clerk, gentle-mannered and seemingly content, suddenly threw his cards down and said: "What am I doing here?"

At first this sentence seemed part of the game, annoyance at some little loss, a provocative remark. The game went on for some time longer, without anyone sensing the dynamite about to explode.

Suddenly the man rose to his feet and said: "What am I doing here?"

"What do you mean, what are you doing here?" they said. "You're playing cards."

"I'm a murderer," he said, not in anger, but with a kind of quiet deliberation, as if the scream in his throat had turned, within a short space of time, to a clear admission of guilt.

"Don't talk like that," they said.

"You know it better than I do," he said. "You'll be my witnesses when the time comes."

"Of course we'll be your witnesses. Of course we will."

"You'll say that Zigi Baum is a murderer."

"That you can't expect of us."

"I, for one, don't intend hiding anything."

This exchange, proceeding without anger, in a matter-of-fact tone, turned gradually into a menacing confrontation.

"You won't tell the truth, then?"

"Of course we'll tell the truth."

"A man abandons his wife and children, his father and his mother. What is he if not a murderer?" He raised his head and a smile broke out on his face. Now he looked like a man who had done what had to be done and was about to take up his practical duties again. He took off his coat, sat down on the ground, and looked around him. He showed no signs of agitation.

For a moment it seemed as if he were about to ask a question. All eyes were on him. He bowed his head. They averted their eyes.

"It's not a big thing to ask, I think," he said to himself. "I didn't want to ask you to do it, I don't know if I should have asked you. The day of judgment will come in the end. If not in this world then in the next. I can't imagine life without justice."

He did not seem confused. There was a straightforward kind of matter of factness in his look. As if he wanted to bring a certain matter up for discussion, a matter which had become a little complicated, but not to such an extent that it could not be discussed with people who were close to him.

He took his tobacco out of his pocket, rolled himself a cigarette, lit it and inhaled the smoke.

Everyone breathed a sigh of relief. He said: "This is good tobacco. It's got the right degree of moisture. You remember how we used to fight over cigarette stubs? We lost our human image. Pardon me—do you say human image or divine image?"

"Neither," said a voice from behind.

This remark was apparently not to his liking. He clamped his teeth on the cigarette and passed his hand over his hair. Now you could see how old he was: not more than thirty-five. His cheeks were slightly lined, his nose was straight, and his ears were set close to his head. There was a concentrated look in his eyes.

"How much do I owe?" he asked one of the others. "I lost, I think."

"It's all written down. You'll pay us back later."

"I don't like being in debt. How much do I owe?"

There was no response. He inhaled and blew the smoke out downward. "Strange," he said. "The war is over. I never imagined it would end like this."

Darkness fell and the tension relaxed. Zigi looked slightly ashamed of the scandal he had caused.

And while they were all sitting there, Zigi rose to his feet, stretched his arms, and raised his knees as if he were about to run a race. In the camp too he had been in the habit of taking short runs, in order to warm himself up. They had saved him then from depression.

Now it seemed as if he were about to take a run, as in the old days. One, two, he said, and set out. He ran six full rounds, and on the seventh he rose into the air and with a broad, slow movement cast himself into the water.

For a moment they all stood rooted to the spot. Then they all rushed together to the single hurricane lamp and stood waving it in the air. "Zigi, Zigi," they cried. A few of them jumped into the river.

All night long they labored in the icy water.

Some of them swam far out, but they did not find Zigi.

And when morning broke the river was smooth and placid. A greenish-blue light shone on its surface. No one spoke. They spread their clothes out to dry and the old moldy smell, which seemed to have gone away, rose once more into the air.

Afterward they lit a fire and sat down to eat. Their hunger was voracious. The loaves of bread disappeared one after the other.

Tzili forgot herself for a moment. Zigi's athletic run went on flashing past her eyes, with great rapidity. It seemed to her that he would soon rise from the river, shake the water off his body, and announce: "The river's fine for swimming."

In the afternoon the place suddenly seemed confined and threatening, the light oppressive. The peasant women came and spread their wares on their flowered cloths, but no one bought anything. The women sat and looked at them with watchful eyes. One of them asked: "Why aren't you buying today? We have bread and smoked meat. Fresh milk too."

"Let's go," someone said, and immediately they all stood up. Tzili too raised her heavy body from the ground. No one asked: "Where to?" A dumb wonder stared from their faces, as after enduring grief. Tzili was glad that the haversack was empty, and now she had nothing but her own body to carry.

29

They walked along the riverside, toward the south. The sun shone on the green fields. Now it seemed that Zigi Baum was floating on the current, his arms outspread. Every now and then his image was reflected on the surface of the water. No one stopped to gaze at this shining reflection. The current widened as it approached the dam, a mighty torrent of water.

Later on a few people turned off to the right. They turned off together, without asking any questions or saying good-by. Tzili watched them walk away. They showed no signs of anger or of happiness. They went on walking at the same pace— for some reason, in another direction.

Tzili, it appeared, was already in the sixth month of her pregnancy. Her belly was taut and heavy but her legs, despite the difficulties of the road, walked without stumbling. When the refugees stopped to rest, they ate in silence. The strange disappearance of Zigi Baum had infected them with a subtle terror, unlike anything they had experienced before.

Tzili was happy. Not a happiness which had any outward manifestations: the fetus stirring inside her gave her an appetite and a lust for life. Not so the others: death clung even to their clothes. They tried to shake it off by walking.

From time to time they quickened their pace and Tzili fell behind. They were as absorbed in themselves now as they had been before in their card game. No one asked: "Where is she?" but nevertheless Tzili felt that their closeness to her was stronger than their distraction.

She no longer thought much about Mark. As if he had set out on a long journey from which it would take a long time to return. He appeared to her now as a tiny figure on the distant horizon, beyond the reach of her voice. She still loved him, but with a different kind of love. A love which had no real taste. From time to time a kind of awe descended on her and she knew: it was Mark, watching her—not uncritically—from afar.

She would say: Mark is inside me, but she didn't really feel it. The fetus was now hers, a secret which no one but she could touch.

Once, when they had stopped to rest, a woman asked her: "Isn't it hard for you?"

"No," said Tzili simply.

"And do you want the baby?"

"Yes."

The woman was surprised by Tzili's reply. She looked at her as if she were some stupid, senseless creature. Then she was sorry and her expression changed to one of wonder and pity: "How will you bring it up?"

"I'll keep it with me all the time," said Tzili simply.

Tzili too wanted to ask: "Where are you from?" But she had learned not to ask. On their last halt a quarrel had broken out between two women as a result of a tactless question. People were very tense and questions brought their repressed anger seething to the surface.

"How old are you?" asked the woman.

"Fifteen."

"So young." Wonder softened the woman's face.

Tzili offered her a piece of bread and she said, "Thank you."

"I," said the woman, "have lost my children. It seems to me that I did everything I could, but they were lost anyway. The oldest was nine and the youngest seven. And I am alive, as you see, even eating. Me they didn't harm. I must be made of iron."

A pain shot through Tzili's diaphragm and she closed her eyes.

"Don't you feel well?" asked the woman.

"It'll pass," said Tzili.

"Give me your mug and I'll fetch you some water."

When the woman returned Tzili was already sitting calmly on the ground. The woman raised the cup to Tzili's mouth and Tzili drank. The woman now wanted more than anything to help Tzili, but she did not know how. Tzili, in spite of everything, had more food than she did.

Straight after this night fell and the woman sank to the ground and slept. She shrank to the size of a child of six. Tzili wanted to cover the woman with her tattered coat, but she immediately suppressed this impulse. She did not want to frighten her.

The others were awake but passive. The isolated words which fluttered in the air were as inward as a conversation between two lovers, no longer young.

The night was warm and fine and Tzili remembered the little yard at home, where she had spent so many hours. Every now and then her mother would call, "Tzili," and Tzili would reply, "Here I am." Of her entire childhood, only this was left. All the rest was shrouded in a heavy mist. She was seized by longing for the little yard. As if it were the misty edge of the Garden of Eden.

"I have to eat." She banished the vision and immediately put her hand into the haversack and tore off a piece of bread. The bread was dry. A few gains of coal were embedded in its bottom crust. She liked the taste of the bread. Afterward she ate a little smoked meat. With every bite she felt her hunger dulled.

30

The summer took them by surprise, hot and broad, filling them with a will to live. The paths all flowed together into green creeks, bordered by tall trees. Refugees streamed from all directions, and for some reason the sight recalled summer holidays, youth movements, seasonal vacations, all kinds of forgotten youthful pleasures. Words from the old lexicon floated in the air. Only their clothes, like an eternal disgrace, went on steaming.

Tzili sat still, this happiness made her anxious. Soon it would give way to screams, pain, and despair.

That night they made a fire, sang and danced, and drank. And as after every catastrophe: embraces, couplings, and despondency in their wake. Tall women with the traces of an old elegance still clinging to them lay sunbathing shamelessly next to the lake.

"What does it matter—there's no point in living anymore anyway," a woman who had apparently run wild all night confessed. She was strong and healthy, fit to bring many more children into the world.

"And you won't go to Palestine?" asked her friend.

"No," said the woman decisively.

"Why not?"

"I want to go to hell."

From this conversation Tzili absorbed the word "Palestine." Once when her sister Yetty had become involved with the Moravian officer, there had been talk of sending her to Palestine. At first Yetty had refused, but then she changed her mind and wanted to go. But by then they didn't have the money to send her. Now Tzili thought often of her sister Yetty. Where was she now?

Tzili's fears were not in vain. The calamities came thick and fast: one woman threw herself into the lake and another swallowed poison. The marvelous oblivion was gone in an instant and the same healthy woman, the one who had refused to go to Palestine, announced: "Death will follow us all our lives, wherever we go. There'll be no more peace for us."

In the afternoon the body was recovered from the lake and the funerals took place one after the other. One of the men, who had the look of a public official even in his rags, spoke at length about the great obligations which were now facing them all. He spoke about memory, the long memory of the Jewish people, the eternal life of the tribe, and the historic necessity of the return to the motherland. Many wept.

After the funeral there was a big argument and the words of the official were heard again. It appeared that the woman who had taken poison had taken it because of a broken promise: someone who wanted to sleep with her had promised to marry her, and the next day he had changed his mind. The woman, who in all the years of suffering had kept the poison hidden in the lining of her coat without using it, had used it now. And something else: before taking the poison the woman had announced her intention of taking it, but no one had believed her.

Now there was nothing left but to say: Because of one night in bed a person commits suicide? So what if he slept with her? So what if he promised her? What do we have left but for the little pleasures of life? Do we have to give those up too?

Tzili took in the words with her eyes shut. She understood the words now, but she did not justify any of them in her heart. She sensed only one thing: the grief which had washed through her too had now become empty and pointless.

31

Now they streamed with the sun toward the sea. And at night they grilled silver fish, fresh from the river, on glowing coals. The nights were warm and clear, bringing to mind a life in which pleasures were real.

There was no lack of quarrels in this mixture. The summer sun worked its magic. As if the years in the camps had vanished without a trace. A forgetfulness which was not without humor. Like, for example, the woman who performed night after night, singing, reciting, and exposing her thighs. No one reminded her of her sins in the labor camp. She was now their carnival queen.

Now too there were those who could not stand the merriment and left. There was no lack of prosecutors, accusers, stirrers up of the past, and spoilsports. At this time too, the first visionaries appeared: short, ardent men who spoke about the salvation of the soul with extraordinary passion. You couldn't get away from them. But the desire to forget was stronger than all these. They ate and drank until late at night.

"What are you doing here?" A man would accost her from time to time, but on seeing that she was pregnant he would withdraw at once and leave her alone.

Tzili was very weak now. The long march had worn her out. From time to time a pain would pierce her and afterward she would feel giddy. Her legs swelled up too, but she bit her lips and said nothing. She was proud that her legs bore her and her baby. For some reason she believed that if her legs were healthy no harm would befall her.

And her life narrowed down to little worries. She forgot everyone and if she remembered them it was casually and absentmindedly. She was with herself, or rather with her body, which kept her occupied day and night. Sometimes someone offered her a piece of fish or bread. When she was very hungry she would stretch out her hand and beg. She wasn't ashamed to beg.

Without anyone noticing, the green creeks turned into a green plain dotted with little lakes. The landscape was so lovely that it hurt, but people were so obsessed with their merrymaking that they took no notice of the change. After a night of drinking they would sleep.

The convoy proceeded slowly and at a ragged pace. Sometimes a sudden panic took hold of them and made them run. Tzili limped after them with the last of her strength. They traipsed from place to place as if they were at the mercy of their changing moods. At this time fate presented Tzili with a moment of peace. Everything was full of joy—the light and the water and her body bearing her baby within it—but not for long.

During one of the panic flights she felt she could not go on. She tried to get up but immediately collapsed again. But for the fat woman, the one who sang and recited and bared her thighs—but for her and the fact that she noticed Tzili's absence and immediately cried: "We've left the child behind"—they would have gone on without her. At first no one paid any attention to her cry, but she was determined to be heard. She called out again, with a kind of authority, like a woman used to raising her voice, and the convoy drew to a halt.

No one knew what to do. During the years of the war they had learned to run and to stop for no one. The fat woman made them stop. "Man is not an insect. This time no one will shirk his duty." A sudden shame covered their faces.

There was no doctor among them, but there was a man who had been a merchant in peacetime and claimed that he had once taken a course in first aid, and he said: "We'll have to carry her on a stretcher." Strange: the words did their work at once. One of them went to fetch wood and another rope, and the skinny merchant, who never opened his mouth, knelt down and with movements that were almost prayerful he joined and he knotted. And they produced a sheet too, and a ragged blanket, and even some pins and some hooks. By nightfall the merchant could survey his handiwork and say: "She'll be quite comfortable on this."

And the next day when the stretcher bearers lifted the stretcher onto their shoulders and set out at the head of the convoy, a mighty song burst from their throats. A rousing sound, like pent up water bursting from a dam. "We are the torch bearers," roared the stretcher bearers, and everyone else joined in.

They carried the stretcher along the creeks and sang. The summer, the glorious summer, turned every corner golden. Tzili herself closed her eyes and tried to make the giddiness go away. The merchant urged the stretcher bearers on: "Run, boys, run. The child needs a doctor." All his anxieties gathered together in his face. And when they stopped he would sit next to her and feed her. He bought whatever he could lay his hands on, but to Tzili he gave only milk products and fruit. Tzili had lost her appetite.

"Thank you," said Tzili.

"There's no reason to thank me."

"Why not?"

"What else have I got to do?" His eyes opened and in the white of the left eye a yellow stain glittered. His despair was naked.

"You're helping me."

"What of it?"

And Tzili stopped thanking him.

At night he would fold his legs and sleep at her side. And Tzili was suddenly freed of the burden of her survival. The stretcher bearers took turns carrying her from place to place. There was not a village or a town to be seen, only here and there a house, here and there a farmer.

"Where are you from?" asked Tzili.

The merchant told her, unwillingly and without going into detail, but he did tell her about Palestine. In his youth he had wanted to go to Palestine. He had spent some time on a Zionist training farm, and he even had a certificate, but his late father had fallen ill and his illness had lasted for years. After that he had married and had children.

There was nothing captivating in the way he spoke. It was evident that he wanted to cut things short in everything concerning himself, like a merchant who put his trust in practical affairs and knew that they took precedence over emotions. Tzili asked no further. He himself left the stretcher only to fetch milk for her. Tzili drank the milk in spite of herself, so that he would not worry.

He never asked: "Where are you from?" or "What happened to you?" He would sit by her side as dumb as an animal. His face was ageless. Sometimes he looked old and clumsy and sometimes as agile as a man of thirty.

167

Once Tzili tried to get off the stretcher. He scolded her roundly. On no account was she to get off the stretcher until she saw a doctor. He knew that this was so from the first aid course.

And the fat woman who had saved Tzili started entertaining them again at night. She would sing and recite and expose her fat thighs. The merchant raised Tzili's head and she saw everything. She felt no affection for any of them, but they were carrying her, taking turns to carry her, from place to place. Between one pain and the next she wanted to say a kind word to the merchant, but she was afraid of offending him. He for his part walked by her side like a man doing his duty, without any exaggeration. Tzili grew accustomed to him, as if he were an irritating brother.

And thus they reached Zagreb. Zagreb was in turmoil. In the yard of the Joint Distribution Committee people were distributing biscuits, canned goods, and colored socks from America. In the courtyard they all mingled freely: visionaries, merchants, moneychangers, and sick people. No one knew what to do in the strange, half-ruined city. Someone shouted loudly: "If you want to get to Palestine, you'd better go to Naples. Here they're nothing but a bunch of money-grubbing profiteers and crooks."

The stretcher bearers put the stretcher down in a shady corner and said: "From now on somebody else can take over." The merchant was alarmed by this announcement and he implored them: "You've done great things, why not carry on?" But they no longer took any notice of him. The sight of the city had apparently confused them. Suddenly they looked tall and ungainly. In vain the merchant pleaded with them. They stood their ground: "From now on it's not our job." The merchant stood helplessly in the middle of the courtyard. There was no doctor present, and the officials of the Joint Committee were busy defending themselves from the survivors, who assailed their caged counters with great force.

If only the merchant had said, "I can't go on anymore," it would have been easier for Tzili. His desperate scurrying about hurt her. But he did not abandon her. He kept on charging into the crowd and asking: "Is there a doctor here? Is there a doctor here?"

People came and went and in the big courtyard, enclosed in a wall of medium height, men and women slept by day and by night. Every now and then an official would emerge and threaten the sleepers or the people besieging the doors. The official's neat appearance recalled other days, but not his voice.

And there was a visionary there too, thin and vacant-faced, who wandered through the crowds muttering: "Repent, repent." People would throw him a coin on condition that he shut up. And he would accept the condition, but not for long.

Pain assailed Tzili from every quarter. Her feet were frozen. The merchant ran from place to place, drugged with the little mission he had taken upon himself. No one came to his aid. When night fell, he put his head between his knees and wept.

In the end a military ambulance came and took her away. The merchant begged them: "Take me, take me too. The child has no one in the whole world." The driver ignored his despairing cries and drove away.

Tzili's pains were very bad, and the sight of the imploring merchant running after the ambulance made them worse. She wanted to scream, but she didn't have the strength.

32

It was a makeshift hospital housed in an army barracks partitioned with blankets. Soldiers and partisans, women and children, lay crowded together. Screams rose from every side. Tzili was placed on a big bed, apparently requisitioned from one of the bombed houses.

For days she had not heard the throbbing of the fetus. Now it seemed to her that it was stirring again. The nurse sponged her down with a warm, wet cloth and asked: "Where are you from?" And Tzili told her. The broad, placid face of the gentile nurse brought her a sudden serenity. It was evident that the young nurse came from a good home. She did her work quietly, without superfluous gestures.

Tzili asked wonderingly: "Where are you from?" "From here," said the nurse. A disinterested light shone from her blue eyes. The nurse told her that every day more soldiers and refugees were brought to the hospital. There were no beds and no doctors. The few doctors there were torn

171

between the hospitals scattered throughout the ruined city.

Later Tzili fell asleep. She slept deeply. She saw Mark and he looked like the merchant who had taken care of her. Tzili told him that she had been obliged to sell all the clothes in the haversack and in the commotion she had lost the haversack too. Perhaps it was with the merchant. "The merchant?" asked Mark in surprise. "Who is this merchant?" Tzili was alarmed by Mark's astonished face. She told him, at length, of all that had happened to her since leaving the mountain. Mark bowed his head and said: "It's not my business anymore." There was a note of criticism in his voice. Tzili made haste to appease him. Her voice choked and she woke up.

The next day the doctor came and examined her. He spoke German. Tzili answered his hurried questions quietly. He told the nurse that she had to be taken to the surgical ward that same night. Tzili saw the morning light darken next to the window. The bars reminded her of home.

They took her to the surgical ward while it was still light. There was a queue and the gentile nurse, who spoke to her in broken German mixed with Slavic words, held her hand. From her Tzili learned that the fetus inside her was dead, and that soon it would be removed from her womb. The anesthetist was a short man wearing a Balaklava hat. Tzili screamed once and that was all.

Then it was night. A long night, carved out of stone, which lasted for three days. Several times they tried to wake her. Medics and soldiers rushed frantically about carrying stretchers. Tzili wandered in a dark stone tunnel, strangers and acquaintances passing before her eyes, clear and unblurred. I'm going back, she said to herself and clung tightly to the wooden handle.

When she woke the nurse was standing beside her. Tzili asked, for some reason, if the merchant too had been hurt. The nurse told her that the operation had not taken long, the doctors were satisfied, and now she must rest. She held a spoon to her mouth.

"Was I good?" asked Tzili.

"You were very good."

"Why did I scream?" she wondered.

"You didn't scream, you didn't make a sound."

In the evening the nurse told her that she had not stirred from the hospital for a whole week. Every day they brought more soldiers and refugees, some of them badly hurt, and she could not leave. Her fiancé was probably angry with her. Her round face looked worried.

"He'll take you back," said Tzili.

"He's not an easy man," confessed the nurse.

"Tell him that you love him."

"He wants to sleep with me," the nurse whispered in her ear.

Tzili laughed. The thin gruel and the conversation distracted her from her pain. Her mind was empty of thought or sorrow. And the pain too grew duller. All she wanted was to sleep. Sleep drew her like a magnet.

33

She fell asleep again. In the meantime the soldiers and refugees crammed the hut until there was no room to move. The medics pushed the beds together and they moved Tzili's bed into the doorway. She slept. Someone strange and far away ordered her not to dream, and she obeyed him and stopped dreaming. She floated on the surface of a vacant sleep for a few days, and when she woke her memory was emptier than ever.

The hut stretched lengthwise before her, full of men, women, and children. The torn partitions no longer hid anything. "Don't shout," grumbled the medics, "it won't do you any good." They were tired of the commotion and of the suffering. The nurses were more tolerant, and at night they would cuddle with the medics or the ambulant patients.

Tzili lay awake. Of all her scattered life it seemed to her that nothing was left. Even her body was no longer hers. A jumble of sounds and shapes flowed into her without touching her.

"Are you back from your leave?" she remembered to ask the nurse.

"I quarreled with my fiancé."

"Why?"

"He's jealous of me. He hit me. I swore never to see him again." Her big peasant hands expressed more than her face.

"And you, did you love him?" she asked Tzili without looking at her.

"Who?"

"Your fiancé."

"Yes," said Tzili, quickly.

"With Jews, perhaps, it's different."

Bitter lines had appeared overnight on her peasant's face. Tzili now felt a kind of solidarity with this country girl whose fiancé had beaten her with his hard fists.

At night the hut was full of screams. One of the medics attacked a refugee and called him a Jewish crook. A sudden dread ran through Tzili's body.

The next day, when she stood up, she realized for the first time that she had lost her sense of balance too. She stood leaning against the wall, and for a moment it seemed to her that she would never again be able to stand upright without support.

"Haven't you seen a haversack anywhere?" she asked one of the medics.

"There's disinfection here. We burn everything."

Women who were no longer young stood next to the lavatories and smeared creams on their faces. They spoke to each other in whispers and laughed provocatively. The years of suffering had bowed their bodies but had not destroyed their will to live. One of the women sat on a bench and massaged her swollen legs with pulling, clutching movements.

Later the medics brought in a lot of new patients. They reclassified the patients and put the ones who were getting better out in the yard.

They put Tzili's bed out too. All the gentile nurses' pleading was in vain.

The next day officials from the Joint Committee came to the yard and distributed dresses and shoes and flowered petticoats. There was a rush on the boxes, and the officials who had come to give things to the women had to beat them off instead. Tzili received a red dress, a petticoat, and a pair of high-heeled shoes. A heavy smell of perfume still clung to the crumpled goods.

"What are you fighting for?" an official asked accusingly.

"For a pretty dress," one of the women answered boldly.

"You people were in the camps weren't you? From you we expect something different," said someone in an American accent.

Later the gentile nurse came and spoke encouragingly to Tzili. "You must be strong and hold your head high. Don't give yourself away and don't show any feelings. What happened to you could have happened to anyone. You have to forget. It's not a tragedy. You're young and pretty. Don't think about the past. Think about the future. And don't get married."

She spoke to her like a loyal friend, or an older sister. Tzili felt the external words spoken by the gentile nurse strengthening her. She wanted to thank her and she didn't know how. She gave her the petticoat she had just received from the Joint Committee. The nurse took it and put it into the big pocket in her apron.

Early in the morning they chased everyone out of the yard.

34

Now everyone streamed to the beach. Fishermen stood by little booths and sold grilled fish. The smell of the fires spread a homely cheerfulness around. Before the war the place had evidently been a jolly seaside promenade. A few traces of the old life still clung to the peeling walls.

Beyond the walls lay the beach, white and spotted with oil stains, here and there an old signpost, a few shacks and boats. Tzili was weak and hungry. There was no familiar face to which she could turn, only strange refugees with swollen packs on their backs and hunger and urgency on their faces. They streamed over the sand to the sea.

Tzili sat down and watched. The old desire to watch came back to her. At night the people lit fires and sang rousing Zionist songs. No one knew how long they would be there. They had food. Tzili too went down to the sea and sat among the refugees. The wound in her stomach was apparently healing. The pain was bad but not unendurable.

"These fish are excellent."

"Fish is good for you."

"I'm going up to buy another one."

These sentences for some reason penetrated into Tzili's head, and she marveled at them.

Somewhere a quarrel broke out. A hefty man shouted at the top of his voice: "No one's going to kill me anymore." Somewhere else people were dancing the hora. One of the refugees sitting next to Tzili remarked: "Palestine's not the place for me."

"Why not?" his friend asked him teasingly.

"I'm tired."

"But you're still strong."

"Yes, but there's no more faith in me."

"And what are you going to do instead?"

"I don't know."

Someone lit an oil lamp and illuminated the darkness. The voice of the refugee died down.

And while Tzili sat watching a fat woman approached her and said: "Aren't you Tzili?"

"Yes," she said. "My name is Tzili."

It was the fat woman who had entertained them on their way to Zagreb, singing and reciting and baring her fleshy thighs.

"I'm glad you're here. They've all abandoned me," she said and lowered her heavy body to the ground. "With all the pretty shiksas here, what do they need me for?"

"And where are you going to go?" said Tzili
carefully.

"What choice do I have?" The woman's reply
was not slow in coming.

For a moment they sat together in silence.

"And you?" asked the woman.

Tzili told her. The fat woman stared at her, devouring every detail. All the great troubles in-
habiting her great body seemed to make way for a
moment for Tzili's secret.

"I too have nobody left in the world. At first I
didn't understand, now I understand. There's the
world, and there's Linda. And Linda has nobody
in the whole wide world."

One of the officials got onto a box. He spoke in
grand, thunderous words. As if he had a loud-
speaker stuck to his mouth. He spoke of Palestine,
land of liberty.

"Where can a person buy a grilled fish?" said
Linda. "I'm going to buy a grilled fish. The hun-
ger's driving me out of my mind. I'll be right back.
Don't you leave me too."

Tzili was captivated for a moment by the speaker's voice. He thundered about the need for re-
newal and dedication. No one interrupted him. It
was evident that the words had been pent up in
him for a long time. Now their hour had come.

Linda brought two grilled fish. "Linda has to eat.
Linda's hungry." She spoke about herself in the

third person. She held a fish in a cardboard wrapper out to Tzili.

Tzili tasted and said: "It tastes good."

"Before the war I was a cabaret singer. My parents disapproved of my way of life," Linda suddenly confessed.

"They've forgiven you," said Tzili.

"No one forgives Linda. Linda doesn't forgive herself."

"In Palestine everything will be different," said Tzili, repeating the speaker's words.

Linda chewed the fish and said nothing.

Tzili felt a warm intimacy with this fat woman who spoke about herself in the third person.

All night the speakers spoke. Loud words flooded the dark beach. A thin man spoke of the agonies of rebirth in Palestine. Linda did not find these voices to her taste. In the end she could no longer restrain herself and she called out: "We've had enough words. No more words." And when the speaker took no notice of her threats she went and stood next to the box and announced: "This is fat Linda here. Don't anyone dare come near this box. I'm declaring a cease-words. It's time for silence now." She went back and sat down. No one reacted. People were tired, they huddled in their coats. After a few moments she said to herself: "Phooey. This rebirth makes me sick."

That same night they were taken aboard the

ship. It was a small ship with a bare mast and a chimney. Two projectors illuminated the shore.

"What I'd like now," said Tzili for some reason, "is a pear."

"Linda hasn't got a pear. What a pity that Linda hasn't got a pear."

"I feel ashamed," said Tzili.

"Why do you feel ashamed?"

"Because that's what came into my head."

"I have every respect for such little wishes. Linda herself is all one little wish."

For the time being the sight was not an inspiring one. People climbed over ropes and tarpaulins. Someone shouted: "There's a queue here, no one will get in without waiting in the queue."

The crush was bad and Tzili felt that pain was about to engulf her again. Linda no longer waited for favors and in a thunderous voice she cried: "Make way for the girl. The girl has undergone an operation." No one moved. Linda shouted again, and when no one paid any attention she spread out her arms and swept a couple of young men from their places on a bench.

"Now, in the name of justice, she'll sit down. Her name is Tzili."

Later on, when the commotion had died down and some of the people had gone down to the cabins below and a wind began to blow on the deck, Tzili said: "Thank you."

"What for?"

"For finding me a place."

"Don't thank me. It's your place."

Afterward shouts were heard from below. People were apparently beating the informers and collaborators in the dark, and the latter were screaming at the tops of their voices. Up on the deck, too, there was no peace. In vain the officials tried to restore order.

Between one scream and the next Linda told Tzili what had happened to her during the war. She had a lover, a gentile estate owner who had hidden her in his granaries. She moved from one granary to another. At first she had a wonderful time, she was very happy. But later she came to realize that her lover was a goy in every sense of the word, drunk and violent. She was forced to flee, and in the end she fled to a camp. She didn't like the Jews, but she liked them better than the gentiles. Jews were sloppy but not cruel. She was in the camp for a full year. She learned Yiddish there, and every night she performed for the inmates. She had no regrets. There was a kind of cruel honesty in her brown eyes.

The little ship strained its engines to cross the stormy sea. Up on the deck they did not feel it rock. Most of the day the passengers slept in the striped coats they had been given by the Joint Committee. From time to time the ship sounded its horn.

Linda managed to get hold of a bottle of brandy at last, and her joy knew no bounds. She hugged the bottle and spoke to it in Hungarian. She started drinking right away, and when her heart was glad with brandy she began to sing. The songs she sang were old Hungarian lullabies.